Contents

Student-Led Devotions for Youth Ministry, Volume 2

Group

Loveland, Colorado

Student-Led Devotions for Youth Ministry, Volume 2

Copyright © 1998 Group Publishing, Inc.

Visit our Web site: **www.grouppublishing.com**

Thanks to all the authors and editors of the great lessons in Group's Active Bible Curriculum® from which this book was compiled.

Credits
Book Acquisitions Editor: Amy Simpson
Editors: Stephen Parolini and Helen Turnbull
Creative Development Editor: Dave Thornton
Chief Creative Officer: Joani Schultz
Copy Editor: Julie Meiklejohn
Art Director: Ray Tollison
Cover Art Director: Jeff A. Storm
Cover Designer: Diana Walters
Cover Photography: Tony Stone Images
Designer: Jean Bruns
Computer Graphic Artist: Joyce Douglas
Illustrator: Sam Thiewes
Production Manager: Gingar Kunkel

Library of Congress Cataloging-in-Publication Data
Student-led devotions for youth ministry, vol. 2
          p.   cm.
1. Church group work with teenagers
BV4447.S728   1998
259'.23—dc21
ISBN 0-7644-2004-6 (v. 1)
ISBN 0-7644-2005-4 (v. 2)

97-52301
CIP

10 9 8 7 6 5   07 06 05 04 03 02

Printed in the United States of America.

Introduction

Ever wonder how to bridge the generation gap with your kids? Do they lose interest during meetings or miss the point of your activities? Ever wonder if *you* really got the point of a lesson or activity? Then maybe it's time to let someone else lead!

This collection of forty-four student-led devotions is designed to help teenagers to get the point by immersing them in experiences that help bring the point to life. Like many Group books, *Student-Led Devotions for Youth Ministry, Volume 2* uses active learning to help the group members understand and apply the message of the activity.

Active learning leads students in doing things that help them understand important principles, messages, and ideas. It's a discovery process that helps kids internalize what they learn. Active learning means learning by doing. And there's no better way for your kids to learn about responsibility, decision-making, and leadership than by leading devotions themselves.

Each activity in this book includes an experience designed to evoke specific feelings in the students. The activities also process those feelings through "How did you feel?" or "What was that like?" questions and apply the message to situations that kids face.

Dive into the activities with your group members. Don't be a spectator; be sure to participate as one of the students. Make sure you plan ahead with your student-leader so he or she will have plenty of time to prepare. And be prepared to answer questions your student-leader may have ahead of time. You may want to photocopy the "Tips for Leading Devotions" handout (p. 6) for your student-leader to give him or her some ideas on how to use these devotions.

And be sure to check out the Scripture and Topical Indexes (pp. 121-122) for a quick survey of what's included in these learning experiences.

If you're looking for activities that you and your kids will remember, look no further: *Student-Led Devotions for Youth Ministry, Volume 2* is your resource.

Tips for Leading Devotions

Plan Ahead

Preparation is essential in making your devotion run smoothly. Be sure you do all these things before you lead your devotion:

● Carefully read through the devotion ahead of time.

● Work with your youth leader to determine how much time you'll need and how much time you're allotted. Practice your devotion so you can be sure to stay on schedule.

● Be sure you have all the supplies needed for the lesson.

● Use a bookmark for the Scriptures you'll use so you can refer to them quickly when necessary.

● Anticipate where you'll need extra help, and designate volunteers before you begin.

● Determine how many students you'll have for your devotion, and adjust the activities accordingly.

Personalize the Devotion

You don't have to read the devotion word-for-word unless you're more comfortable doing that. If you feel the need to change an activity slightly to suit your needs, be sure to check with your youth leader to make sure your changes are appropriate.

Pick a devotion you're interested in, and read up on the subject. You also might want to gather magazine articles, books, or music that are relevant to your subject and incorporate them into your devotion.

Follow Up With Discussion

An important part of leading a devotion is asking thought-provoking questions. Always make sure you have time for the discussion questions that follow an activity. Encourage everyone to participate, but don't force students to respond if they seem uncomfortable.

Sometimes you may only need to ask one question to have a good discussion. At other times, you may have to ask a lot of questions and prompt answers. In these cases, use the possible responses that follow each question to help generate a good discussion.

Across the Line

Purpose:
Students will explore ways to overcome obstacles to reaching out to people who are different from them.

Supplies:
You'll need a Bible and masking tape.

Experience:

Form two teams, and have them face each other across a masking tape line on the floor. Tell kids you're going to play a game similar to Tug of War, but the object of this game is for each person to try to pull individual members from the opposing team across the line onto his or her team. Once a player is pulled across the line, he or she must switch teams and start helping the new team win. Remind kids not to be too rough. Play until everyone is on one team. Ask:

● **What did you like most about this game?** *(The excitement; getting people onto my side of the boundary.)*

● **What did you like least?** *(Changing teams; people not switching teams when they were supposed to.)*

● **How did it feel when you were pulled onto the other team's side?** *(It was hard to adjust; I was glad because my friends were on the other team already.)*

● **How is this game like making friends?** *(You have to reach out; sometimes you have to cross a boundary to meet new people.)*

● **What were obstacles or boundaries that kept you from pulling people over to your team?** *(They didn't want to move; others helped them stay on their side.)*

● **What are obstacles or boundaries that discourage you from making new friends?** *(Social status; race; language.)*

Say: **Making friends with people who are different from you is a lot like playing this game. At first we were divided on opposing sides of the boundary. But as each person reached out and pulled someone across, we eventually became one team. It's a game that has no losers.**

If your group is racially diverse, be sensitive to kids' feelings following this activity. You may discover that students have "obstacles" that keep them from getting along with other group members. If appropriate, discuss kids' feelings and try to help them see the value in breaking down the racial barriers.

Say: **Sometimes it's difficult to cross barriers to make new friends. God commanded Jonah to cross cultural barriers to reach out to new people, but Jonah resisted.**

Read aloud the story of Jonah in Jonah 1:1–2:1 and 2:1–3:10. Then form groups of no more than four. Have the students in each group create and perform a skit telling this story using a modern-day experience as if it happened to them instead of to Jonah. For example, a group might create a skit in which a student was supposed to reach out to a new foreign-exchange student but didn't want to.

As groups design their skits, have them discuss these questions:

● **What nation or group of people would you choose as your "Nineveh"?**

● **Where would you run to get away from God?**

● **What would God have to do to get you to obey him?**

When groups are ready, have each group perform its skit. Then ask:

● **What did you learn from placing yourself in this story?** *(It helped me understand how Jonah must have felt; I learned I would probably respond just like Jonah did.)*

● **What kinds of feelings would you have if God really asked you to do the action that you performed in the skit?** *(Fear; anger.)*

● **How are people today like Jonah?** *(They still try to run from God; they're still afraid to reach out to new people.)*

● **What people are difficult for you to reach out to? Why?** *(People who aren't Christians; people who are disabled; people who act different.)*

Say: **God asks us to reach out to people from other places even if we disagree with them. And just like Jonah, we must overcome our fears and trust that God will be with us as we reach out to others.**

Bean Bargain

Purpose:

Kids will explore ways to handle conflict.

Supplies:

You'll need Bibles, ten dried beans for each group member, a candy bar (or a similar food prize that kids would like), newsprint, tape, a marker, pencils, coins, and a "Happy-Ending Replay" handout (p. 12) for each person. Before the lesson, write the following list on newsprint:

1. I win, you lose. (Fight)

2. I want out; I withdraw. (Avoid)

3. I give in to keep the peace. (Surrender)

4. I'll meet you halfway. (Compromise)

5. I'll go through it with you; we'll work on the problem together. (Resolve)

Experience:

Give kids each ten dried beans and then display the prize you've brought. The instructions you'll give for this game will be intentionally brief and vague.

Say: **Here's the grand prize. Whoever has the most beans at the end of two minutes wins. Ready? Set? Go!**

Many of the students will want more instruction. Others will start into the competition on their own terms. Just keep looking at your watch. The activity is deliberately open-ended to let students experience how they deal with the conflicts they feel between the need to win and the need to know the rules and play fairly.

It's likely some students will aggressively confront others to get their beans, some will choose negotiation, and others will withdraw. The situation is one of inherent conflict based on each person's need to have something that others are unwilling to give up.

If you feel the activity is growing too aggressive, call time early or ask the aggressive players to sit down and forfeit their beans.

When the two minutes are up, total each person's beans, declare the winner (or winners), and award the winner the prize. Ask:

● **How is the way you felt during this game like the way you feel when you're in a conflict in real life?** *(I feel angry when I'm in fights; I feel defensive when someone disagrees with me.)*

● **What was the problem with this game?** *(I didn't know what to do; I couldn't believe you didn't explain it more.)*

● **What methods did you use to try to get what you needed?** *(I just grabbed for other people's beans; I tried to make a deal to share the prize; I just tried to hang on to my own beans.)*

● **What, if anything, happened in this game that made you angry?** *(Some people got really pushy; I was mad because I didn't know what to do.)*

● **What did you do when you got angry?** *(I started fighting back; I dropped out of the game.)*

● **How many of you tried to get beans by intimidating other students? by negotiating? by working with others to gang up on somebody?**

● **How is this game like real life?** *(Some people will do anything to get what they want; it's a dog-eat-dog world.)*

● **What rules for playing the game seemed to be accepted by most of this group?** *(It was OK to go for the beans as long as you didn't get too rough.)*

Say: **Since we're looking at conflict in this session, it's important to realize from the beginning that conflict is a result of people trying to meet their own needs.**

In this activity, you saw people react to conflict in different ways. People who have made a study of conflict-resolution styles say there are five main ways people deal with conflict.

Take the newsprint you prepared before the study, and tape it to a wall.

Say: **Take a moment to think about which style you used in this conflict situation.** Ask:

● **What do you think your typical conflict-resolution style might be?** *(I'm definitely a fighter; I usually withdraw; I like to work it out.)*

Say: **We all have our own natural ways of dealing with conflict, but what we do naturally isn't always the best thing. The Bible has some interesting things to teach us about conflict. Let's take a look.**

Give students each a photocopy of the "Happy-Ending Replay" handout (p. 12), a pencil, and a Bible. Form pairs, and have each pair flip a coin to determine who will take the role of Cain and who will be Abel. Give the pairs a few minutes to work through the handout.

Then bring the group together. Ask students to share their problem-solving ideas for Cain and Abel. Then ask:

● **What needs did Cain have that resulted in his action against Abel?** *(The need to be accepted by God; the need to succeed.)*

● **How do you think Cain was feeling just before the murder?** *(Hurt; rejected; put down; jealous.)*

● **What conflict-resolution style best describes Cain's approach to solving his conflict with God and with Abel?** *(Fight—I win, you lose.)*

● **Was it effective? Why or why not?** *(Yes, but he was the loser in the end; no, someone died because of it.)*

Form new pairs. Have one person in each pair be the speaker and the other be the listener. Have speakers each tell their partners about a time they had a "happy ending" to a conflict. Have listeners then tell how their partners did a good job handling the conflict.

For example, a speaker might say, "My sister and I always argued about her wearing my clothes. Now we work it out by deciding at the beginning of the week which clothes we'll share instead of fighting at the last minute." The listener might then respond by saying, "You showed a loving attitude by being willing to share with your sister."

After a minute or two, have listeners and speakers change roles and repeat the activity.

Say: **Conflict resolution happens when people on both sides of a conflict decide to look at the problem objectively and work through it together. It may mean giving up something, but you get a happy ending and a stronger relationship in return.**

Happy-Ending Replay

Read through the story in Genesis 4:1-9 with your partner. Then flip a coin to choose roles: Heads is Cain; tails is Abel. Work through these problem-solving steps to reach a happier ending to the story. Write how you'll deal with each step in the space below.

cain   **Abel**

1. **Describe the problem.** Go to the other person and agree to look at the problem together. No blaming!

2. **Discuss alternative solutions.** How could the problem be solved? No ideas are too weird.

3. **Find areas of agreement.** List the solutions that have appeal to both people.

4. **Develop a course of action.** What steps can you take to resolve the conflict, based on the areas of agreement?

Broken Relationships

Purpose:

Students will explore how reconciliation can heal relationships.

Supplies:

You'll need Bibles, paper, markers, newsprint, tape, and pencils.

Experience:

Provide each student with a sheet of paper and a marker. Say: **Think of the person you love the most. Imagine that your piece of paper represents your relationship with that person. I'm going to ask you to write about that person. You won't need to show your paper to anyone. I'll pause after each item to allow you to write your comments on your paper.** Pause after you read each of the following directions.

- **Write the person's name.**
- **Write about one special time you shared with the person.**
- **Write about a place that's been special in your relationship and tell why it's been special.**
- **Describe a meaningful gift the person has given you.**
- **Tell something you're especially thankful for about the person.**
- **Write three words that describe the best qualities of the person.**

Ask students each to look at his or her paper and imagine that it represents this wonderful relationship. Read the following list of instructions, and ask kids to follow each instruction if it applies to the relationship. Say:

- **If the person has ever disappointed you, tear your paper in half.**
- **If the person has ever said something that hurt your feelings (even slightly), tear your paper again.**
- **If the person has ever failed to keep a promise, tear your paper again.**
- **Has that person ever been unavailable when you needed him or her? If so, tear your paper again.**

• If that person has ever been angry with you, tear your paper again.

Ask:

• **What thoughts did you have about your piece of paper when you were asked to imagine it represented an important relationship?** *(It really became important to me; I wasn't able to imagine that.)*

• **How difficult was it to tear the paper when you were asked to?** *(It was very hard because it represented a special relationship; it wasn't any big deal; I didn't really want to.)*

• **What are your reactions when you look at your torn paper?** *(I feel sad; I'm disappointed; it makes me feel uncomfortable.)*

• **How is that like the way you feel when you think about a close friendship that's been damaged or broken?** *(I feel upset about it; it isn't; I'd feel much worse.)*

• **How was the experience you just had like problems you may have in close relationships?** *(It isn't; sometimes problems cause tears in a relationship.)*

Provide students with tape, and ask them to tape their papers back together. Ask:

• **How does your taped paper compare to the paper before it was torn?** *(It's basically the same, but it has tape on it; it doesn't quite look the same.)*

• **How are the taped papers like relationships that have been "repaired"?** *(You still have scars; you can fix broken relationships.)*

• **How is taping your paper back together like repairing a relationship?** *(It's not; it's hard to put your relationship back together after you've ripped it; a relationship may never be the same.)*

Say: **Just as we can tell our papers were once ripped, scars often remain when relationships are repaired after having been broken. But as we can discover from the Bible, reconciliation can only help build relationships.**

Form groups of no more than five and assign each group one of the following passages: Matthew 18:21-35 or Romans 12:14-19. Give groups each a sheet of paper, a pencil, and a Bible.

Ask groups to read their Scripture passages and list on their paper principles they find in the Bible about relating to other people. After groups finish, ask them to share what they've written.

Groups with the Matthew passage might list things such as, "Be sincere about forgiveness" or "Always forgive others."

Groups with the Romans passage might list things such as, "Bless those who wrong you," "Don't be conceited," "Live at peace with everyone," and "Don't take revenge."

Have a volunteer read aloud Romans 12:18. Ask:

● **What does this verse mean?** *(Fix all the problems you have with others; don't make enemies.)*

● **Whose responsibility is it to make peace in broken relationships?** *(The person who's been wronged; the person who's done wrong.)*

● **Should you forgive people who aren't repentant? Why or why not?** *(Yes, Jesus forgave us even though we didn't repent; no, we should only forgive when people ask for forgiveness.)*

● **Does "making peace" mean you must sacrifice your morals or beliefs? Explain.** *(No, you shouldn't make peace if you have to sacrifice your beliefs; maybe, if the relationship is important to you.)*

Say: **It's our responsibility to make peace; it's not enough to wait for someone else to apologize. But making peace with someone doesn't mean we have to sacrifice our morals or convictions. For example, you could make peace by joining friends in making fun of someone else, but that's not what Paul meant.**

Let's look at a Bible story of someone who chose to make peace with his brother. Esau had not seen Jacob for years. In fact, the last time Esau had seen Jacob, Jacob had cheated him in order to gain their father's blessing. Before Jacob finally returned to see Esau, he sent him many gifts, hoping to appease his brother.

Ask a student to read aloud Genesis 33:1-12. Then tape a sheet of newsprint to the wall and give students each a marker. (If you have more than ten people in your group, use one sheet of newsprint for every six to eight people.) Ask students to write or draw on the newsprint words or things that represent how the reunion between Jacob and Esau might have felt.

Say: **Reunions are usually happy times where people freely give out compliments and words of encouragement to each other. Let's see what that might feel like.**

Have students each go around and tell at least two other people one thing they appreciate about those people. For example, students might say, "I appreciate your sense of humor" or "I enjoy listening to your good ideas." Then ask:

● **How did you feel hearing these compliments?** *(I felt good; I felt uncomfortable; I liked it.)*

● **How is that like the way you feel when you've reconciled with someone after a break in your relationship?** *(It's similar, I feel good when I get close to a friend again; it's similar, I feel uncomfortable about reconciliation.)*

Have students list on the newsprint how they feel when reconciliation takes place. Keep the newsprint up in the room for a few weeks as a reminder of the importance of reconciliation in relationships.

Build Up or Break Down

Purpose:

Students will examine how positive communication can help build better relationships with parents.

Supplies:

You'll need Bibles; enough copies of the "+ and - Cards" handout (p. 18) so each group of four can have twenty "+" cards and ten "-" cards; scissors; blocks made of wood, cardboard, or plastic; newsprint; tape; markers; and paper. Before class, cut out the cards and separate them into piles for each group.

Experience:

Form groups of four. Give groups each twenty "+" cards and ten "-" cards from the "+ and - Cards" handout (p. 18) and twenty blocks. Have groups each shuffle their cards.

Have each group form a circle. Say: **In your group, use the cards and the blocks to build a block tower. The rules are simple: Going clockwise, take turns drawing cards. If you draw a "+" card, add a block to the tower. If you draw a "-" card, take a block away from the tower. If you draw a "-" card first, just keep drawing until you draw a "+" card. You have one minute.**

Call time before any group goes through all its cards. Then have groups compare towers. Ask:

● **What went through your mind while you were building your tower?** *(I felt discouraged; I was anxious.)*

● **What were your thoughts when you got a "-" card?** *(I was angry; I was disappointed.)*

● **Did you work well with other group members? Why or why not?** *(No, I wanted to build the tower differently; yes, we worked as a team.)*

● **How is building a tower like communicating with your parents?** *(It takes time for it to be established; every part of the tower is important, so* *everything you say is important.)*

● **How is a "-" card like bad communication with parents?** *(It takes away what's already been built; it hurts the relationship.)*

Say: **You can say things that help and build up others, or you can tear others down with your words. Let's look at several building blocks for positive communication with your parents.**

Write the words from Ephesians 4:25 on a sheet of newsprint, and tape the newsprint to the wall. Read aloud the verse and then ask:

● **What building blocks of good communication do you see in this verse?** *(Don't lie; we belong to each other.)*

● **How could we sum up this verse in one word or phrase?** *(Tell the truth; be united.)*

Form five groups. (A group can be one person.) Give each person a Bible, and assign each group a different verse from the following: Leviticus 19:3; Ephesians 4:25; Ephesians 4:29; Ephesians 4:32; and 1 Peter 2:17. Give groups each several sheets of paper and a marker.

Say: **Read your assigned verse. Then pick out key words, phrases, or themes about good communication. Write one key word, phrase, or theme on each sheet of paper. Then tear your paper to form building-block shapes.**

When groups are finished, have them each explain what they wrote. Then have groups tape their paper building-blocks to the wall to form one large tower.

Call everyone together, and distribute more paper. Have students brainstorm words and phrases that mean the opposite of the building-block words they taped to the wall. As students share, have volunteers write each response on a separate sheet of paper and then tear each sheet of paper to form a star burst shape; use the margin illustration as a guide. Then have volunteers tape the "communication blasters" on top of the paper building-block tower. Ask:

● **How do these communication blasters hurt relationships?** *(They break down trust; they make people angry.)*

● **How does always being honest affect your relationship with your parents?** *(They know they can trust me; it doesn't do any good.)*

● **How does lying affect your relationship with your parents?** *(They're always suspicious; they get mad.)*

Say: **By avoiding communication blasters like those we talked about and practicing honesty and good communication, we can build positive relationships with our parents.**

+ and − Cards

Photocopy and cut apart these cards. Make sure each group
has twenty "+" cards and ten "−" cards.

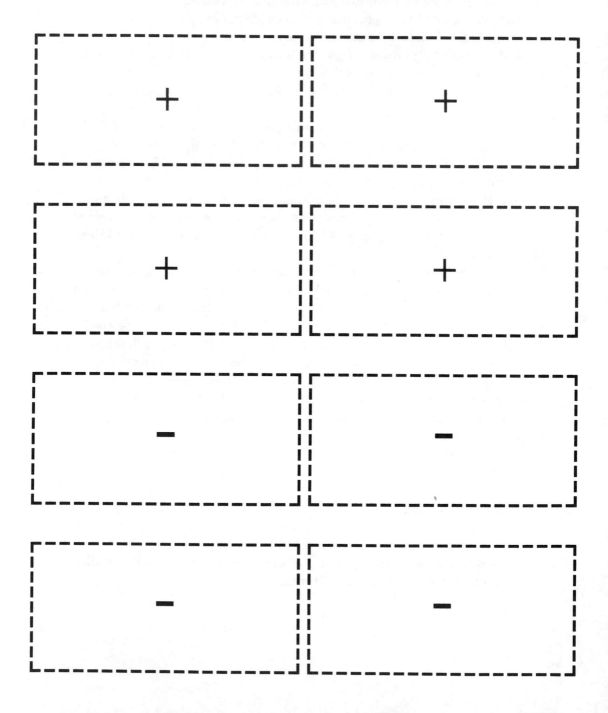

Communication Breakdown

Purpose:

Students will explore ways to work things out when they disagree with friends.

Supplies:

You'll need Bibles, a set of "Communication Breakdown" slips (p. 22) for every two people, paper, pencils, and balloons.

Experience:

Form pairs. Pass out one set of "Communication Breakdown" slips (p. 22) to each pair, and ask each person to take one of the slips. Warn students not to look at their partners' slips or at anyone else's. Give a sheet of paper to each pair.

Say: **Read your slip and then put it in your pocket. You may not see what the other person has on his or her slip. You both have the same basic task to accomplish, but you may not talk. You have a limited time in which to do your task.**

Give your group about three minutes to accomplish the tasks. Then ask:

● **How many of you were able to get your tasks done?** *(Answers will vary.)*

● **What would have helped you to get your task done more effectively?** *(If we'd been able to talk about the things we were supposed to do; if I could have seen the other slip.)*

● **What were your feelings during the exercise?** *(Frustration; confusion.)*

● **How is this activity like conflict in real life?** *(We all want to do things our own way even when we disagree; we get worked up over unimportant things.)*

● **What kind of strategy did you use to get your task done?** *(We didn't get done; we took turns doing the task each other's way.)*

● **How could that same strategy, or a strategy like it, be applied to** real-life situations in which friends disagree? *(Sometimes when you think you're disagreeing, you're just coming at the same thing from different angles; we really need to listen to each other more.)*

● **What do you think causes friends to have disagreements?** *(Lack of communication; wanting to do things differently; assuming the other person agrees with you all the time; not asking how the other person feels.)*

● **How can we avoid the things we just mentioned?** *(Don't assume your friend always wants to do the same thing you do; keep checking with your friends to see what they're feeling and thinking about things.)*

Say: **Try as we might, sometimes things just go wrong between friends.**

Give a slip of paper, a balloon, and a pencil to each student. Depending on the size of your group, you may wish to have the students work in pairs or small groups. On their slips, have students each write a two-sentence description of a disagreement he or she had with a friend, including what it was about and what caused it. Then have students roll up their slips, put them in the balloons, and inflate and tie off the balloons. Put all the balloons in a pile, and allow each student (or group) to choose one balloon that isn't the one he or she placed in the pile. When everyone has a balloon, have students each pop the balloon and come up with a way to resolve the conflict described on the paper.

After all the students have offered their solutions, ask:

● **How did you feel about helping solve someone else's problems?** *(Good; I felt nervous about giving bad advice.)*

● **How different was it from solving your own problems?** *(I felt a lot more levelheaded about someone else's problem than I do about my own; the answer seemed obvious.)*

● **Do you think the answer you gave could really work? Why or why not?** *(Probably, if both sides agree to do it; maybe not, my answer doesn't seem practical.)*

● **Can disagreements between friends ever be good? If so, when?** *(Sometimes yes, when a disagreement keeps a friend from getting into trouble; yes, if a disagreement can help you understand the other person better.)*

Say: **We came up with some interesting ways to resolve these conflicts. But how many of our solutions do you think were solutions God would choose? God has set up ways for us to resolve conflicts. Let's see how close our ideas were to what the Bible suggests we do.**

Have volunteers read aloud Proverbs 27:6; Matthew 5:23-24; and Matthew 18:15-20. Then ask:

● **The verse in Proverbs seems to say that there are times a friend actually does you a favor by hurting you. Can you think of an example?** *(Any time a friend says or does something to keep me from hurting myself; if a friend stops me from doing something that really offends her.)*

● **How would you sum up Jesus' advice in Matthew 5:23-24?** *(Take care of disagreements as quickly as you can; don't pretend that everything's all right if it isn't.)*

● **Why do you think it's so important to work quickly to resolve conflicts with your friends?** *(The longer you wait, the more it hurts your friendship; if you wait, you could start developing a grudge.)*

● **Why do you suppose that Jesus taught in Matthew 18:15-20 to first go directly to someone with whom you have a problem?** *(So you won't talk about that person behind his back; so you won't get other people to not like that person.)*

● **Based on these passages, what happens when friends actually resolve their differences?** *(You can stay friends; you can learn from each other.)*

● **What do you feel is the toughest thing about resolving conflicts with friends?** *(Saying "I'm sorry"; facing the fact that we might never agree about some things.)*

● **How do you feel about Jesus' teaching about conflicts in friendships?** *(It's hard but possible; I don't think I could do it.)*

Say: **Whenever we have a conflict, it's natural to want to withdraw from the person we're arguing with. But Jesus teaches us that nobody wins when we don't try to resolve our conflicts with others. It takes courage. But more than that, it takes love.**

Communication Breakdown

Make enough copies so that every two students will have one set of instructions.

1a. You and your partner must pick one shoe that ties. Your task is to untie and retie the shoe.

- -

1b. You and your partner must pick one shoe that ties. Your task is to untie, unlace, relace, and retie the shoe.

2a. You and your partner may have one sheet of paper. Your task is to fold the paper into four square sections.

- -

2b. You and your partner may have one sheet of paper. Your task is to fold the paper into four triangular sections.

3a. You and your partner must move around the room arm-in-arm. You must go around clockwise on your knees.

- -

3b. You and your partner must move around the room arm-in-arm. You must go around counterclockwise, hopping.

Cookies

Purpose:

Students will examine Christlike ways to face opposition and persecution.

Supplies:

You'll need Bibles, cookies, a plate, two to four copies of the "Cookie Petition" handout (p. 26), paper, and pencils. Before class, set out a plate of about five or six cookies, and place the rest of the cookies out of sight.

Experience:

Show the group the plate of cookies.

Say: **It's a good time for a snack. Unfortunately, I don't have enough cookies for the whole group. So, let's form teams, and I'll give the cookies to one of the teams.**

Form two to four teams. Give each team a photocopy of the "Cookie Petition" handout (p. 26). Tell the students that the first team to have each member sign the petition and turn it in will receive the cookies. Make it clear that every team member must sign the petition or the team isn't eligible to receive the cookies. Also, tell kids that the winning petition will be put in a place of honor at the front of the church for everyone to see.

Tell the students that if no team wins the cookies, the leaders will eat them. Then give the teams a few minutes to go over their handouts and debate whether they'll sign.

If a team seems divided on whether to sign, try to talk kids into signing by either making more promises or threats. If a team gets all its members to sign, tell them you changed your mind and you're going to save the cookies for the leaders to eat after all.

After the exercise, ask:

● **What were your feelings during this activity?** *(I was angry; I was confused; it seemed unfair; I was hungry.)*

● **How did you feel toward your other team members?** *(Like they were uncooperative; like they were trying to make me do something I didn't want to do.)*

● **Have you ever been in a situation similar to this? What did you do?** *(Talked it out; I didn't say anything because I was afraid I'd hurt other people's feelings.)*

● **What are some ways people try to make you compromise something you believe?** *(Peer pressure; advertising; ridicule.)*

Say: **Jesus and his disciples had to face much stronger opposition. Like many people in other countries today, they had to be willing to put their lives on the line for their beliefs.**

Give each person a sheet of paper and a pencil. Ask for a volunteer to read aloud Isaiah 53:7-9.

Say: **In this passage, Isaiah describes the opposition Jesus faced when he walked on the earth. That opposition eventually led to Jesus' crucifixion. I want you to imagine for a minute that you're there at Jesus' crucifixion. Picture the landscape. Smell the air. See the people who are around you. Then write the answers to these questions on your paper:**

● **What is the weather like?**

● **What colors are the people wearing?**

● **What emotions are you feeling as you watch Jesus being placed on the cross?**

● **What would you like to say to Jesus to help him make it through this?**

Give the students a few minutes to write their answers. Then have several students tell what they've written. Ask:

● **What were your thoughts as you were imagining this scene?** *(I felt sad; I wanted to stop them from crucifying Jesus.)*

● **How do you think Jesus' friends reacted to his crucifixion?** *(They went into hiding; they mourned for him; they stayed together.)*

● **What are your reactions toward the authorities who crucified Jesus?** *(They make me angry; I feel like they are cruel; like they should be punished.)*

Have a volunteer read aloud John 15:18-21.

Say: **Well, it is now two thousand years later, but people still hate Jesus. And now they're taking it out on his followers. Imagine you live in a country where Christianity is illegal. Write on your paper the answers to these questions:**

● **Who are your friends?**

● **What do you say when people ask you if you're a Christian?**

● **What would you do if someone offered you a new car to sign a petition stating that Jesus is a liar?**

● **What if they threaten to flunk you out of school if you don't sign?**

● **How far are you willing to go in defense of your faith?**

Again, allow volunteers to tell what they've written.

Say: **We're fortunate to live in a country where Christianity is not illegal. However, we still face opposition to our faith—even here in America.** Ask:

● **What are ways people try to oppose our efforts for Christianity?**

(Make fun of us; exclude us from activities; outlaw prayer in schools.)

● **How do you feel when people make fun of you and other Christians?** *(Mad; nervous; shy.)*

Say: **People who dislike Christianity can do all kinds of things to make life uncomfortable, but they can never take Jesus out of your heart.**

Set out the remainder of the cookies for everyone to enjoy.

Cookie Petition

We, the undersigned, do hereby petition to receive the cookies being offered to our group. In order to be eligible for these cookies, each of us does hereby agree wholeheartedly to the following statement:

I HATE MY PARENTS AND EVERY OTHER PERSON IN THIS GROUP.

Signed,

_____   _____

_____   _____

_____   _____

_____   _____

_____   _____

_____   _____

_____   _____

_____   _____

_____   _____

Crunch!

Purpose:

Students will discover that God gives them the strength to endure hard times.

Supplies:

You'll need Bibles, construction paper, pencils, bathroom tissue, tape, eggs, white vinegar, and "bubble" plastic wrap. Soak one egg in white vinegar for twenty-four hours (make sure this is your egg in the activity).

Experience:

Form teams of three or four, and give each team an egg, a piece of construction paper, and a pencil.

Say: **We're going to have an egg-dropping contest. In an egg-dropping contest, your team has to use the materials here to come up with a protective container to put your egg in. I want you to design your container on paper and explain to us how it works. Then we'll test your ideas by dropping the eggs onto a hard surface from a particular height.**

Limit each team to a few sheets of construction paper, some bathroom tissue, and a small amount of tape. Give your own egg container a secret advantage by putting "bubble" plastic wrap around it and by using an egg that you've soaked in white vinegar for twenty-four hours. (This makes it soft, so it's harder to crack.) Take time before the lesson to test your egg wrapped in bubble wrap to make sure your egg doesn't break.

After teams have their containers put together and their eggs in place, let them explain their designs and proceed with the egg-dropping. Choose an outdoor location where cleanup will be easiest. When all of the eggs have been dropped, gather the group together and ask:

● **How did you come up with your design?** *(We just thought it up; by accident.)*

● **How confident were you with your design?** *(Not very; I knew it wouldn't work.)*

● **How is that like the way you feel when you face a difficult situation in life?** *(I feel hopeless sometimes; I don't even want to go on because I don't think it'll do any good.)*

● **What did you all think about my entry in this contest?** *(I thought* *you had it rigged; you had an unfair advantage.)*

● **How does my participation in this contest relate to real life?** *(You knew what was coming and prepared for it; there are people who cheat; there are people who have a special advantage in life.)*

● **How do you feel about this statement: "If your hope is in Jesus, your hope will never fail"? Explain.** *(I think it's true, because Jesus never fails us; it's true because people who put their hope in anything but Jesus will be let down eventually.)*

● **How are my egg and special container like someone who puts his or her hope in Jesus?** *(You have a strength to face hard times that others don't have; you know you can make it through anything.)*

● **How can you put your hope in God even in hard times?** *(By realizing that he's in control and he loves me; by not trying to solve the problem myself.)*

Say: **Knowing that God gives us the strength to endure hard times is wonderful. But we can look even deeper to discover why God allows the hard times in the first place.**

Pass out Bibles, paper, and pencils, and form three groups. Assign each group one of the following passages: Isaiah 53:1-6; Isaiah 53:7-12; and 2 Corinthians 1:3-7.

Say: **After reading the Scripture aloud in your group, I'd like each of you to list three to five songs that you think have a message that's similar to your passage. It doesn't have to be a perfect match—just pick songs that remind you of the feelings your passage points out. After you list your songs, share them with the members of your group and tell them why you picked the songs you did. Have someone in your group make a list of everyone's songs.**

After about five minutes, call time and bring the group members back together. Ask:

● **What was the first song each of you came up with? Why did you choose that song?** *(Answers will vary.)*

● **What do these songs tell us about these Scripture passages?** *(That people still deal with these issues today; that people's feelings haven't changed much over the years.)*

● **Does your passage make you hopeful or worried? Explain.** *(Hopeful, because it promises God will care for me when I'm down; worried, because God might let me suffer just to help someone else.)*

● **Why do you think God allows his people to suffer?** *(So they can help others; so they can be more like Christ.)*

Say: **God offers a special grace and comfort to his people when they suffer. When we learn to find hope in God in hard times, he is able to change us deep inside to be more like Jesus. In the end, we'll be happier and more able to help others who go through the same things.**

Destination: Chaos

Purpose:

Students will explore how to "fight fair" in conflict situations.

Supplies:

You'll need a Bible, poster board, markers, tape, index cards, yarn, scissors, and one copy of the "Unfair Fighting" handout (p. 32) for each team of six. Before class, write each of the following words on an index card: "ballgame," "movie," "concert," and "party." Make enough cards so each student will have one.

Experience:

Make four poster-board signs, one with each of the following words written on it: "ballgame," "movie," "concert," and "party." Tape one sign on each wall of the room. Tie teams of three to six students together at the ankles with a piece of yarn. Give students each a "destination" card. Explain that students are each to keep their destinations a secret from the other members of their team. Set up a natural conflict situation by giving at least two different destinations to students on the same team.

Say: **Your goal is to get to the destination that's written on your card. You may not talk to anyone or show anyone else your card. You may only communicate using gestures. You have two minutes to arrive at your destination. If any teams break their yarn, they're disqualified. OK, go!**

Chaos is likely to break out as students try to pull their teammates in different directions. Congratulate any team that actually manages to arrive at a destination. Find out who held the cards for that destination, and shake their hands. Then call the teams together for discussion. Ask:

● **What was going through your mind as you were trying to get the other students on your team to move in the direction you wanted to go?** *(I was frustrated at not being able to communicate my desires; I felt I had to push the hardest to get my own way.)*

● **What methods did you use to try to influence your team to move in a particular direction?** *(Pushing; refusing to move; being uncooperative.)*

● **How was this activity like real-life conflicts between friends?** *(Sometimes it's hard to agree on what we're going to do; sometimes it seems like we're pulling in all different directions.)*

● **What methods do you normally use to influence your friends' decisions?** *(I pout until I get my way; I'm good at talking people into doing what I want to do; it seems like I never get my way.)*

● **What kinds of issues can cause fighting among friends?** *(Where to go; what to do; who to invite.)*

Say: **Conflicts among friends are bound to happen simply because people have different needs. The important thing to remember is that there's a right way to fight and a wrong way to fight. Handling conflicts in the right way can build stronger relationships. Handling conflicts in the wrong way can mean the end of a friendship. We need to make an overall commitment to fighting fair. Let's see just what that means.**

Form teams of six. Give each team scissors and one photocopy of the "Unfair Fighting" handout (p. 32). Tell teams to cut the handout into cards, and make sure team members each have one "Foul Card" and one "Loose-Lips Card."

Say: **The object of this game is to match your Foul Cards with the correct Loose-Lips Cards. The person with Foul Card 1 will read it aloud. If you think you have the Loose Lips-Card that demonstrates that unfair-fighting technique, slap the card down on the table (or the floor). Then read it aloud. See if your teammates agree that you have the matching card. If you think you have a match, place the cards side by side on the table (or the floor). Then go on to Foul Card 2. The first team to correctly match all its cards wins.**

The correct matches are 1B, 2E, 3C, 4A, 5D, and 6F.

After the game, say: **Learning how to have a "fair fight" may be one of the most important skills you'll gain in this activity. We can find an interesting example of fair fighting in the Bible. This particular fight was between two influential disciples of Jesus—Peter and Paul. Paul describes the action in Galatians 2:11-14.**

Have a volunteer read the passage aloud. Then ask:

● **What examples of fair fighting can you find in Paul's description of this incident?** *(He spoke directly to Peter instead of behind his back; he focused on one specific issue; he didn't call him names or make unnecessary generalizations.)*

● **Do you think Paul was setting a bad example by allowing this conflict between two prominent church leaders to be seen? Why or why not?** *(No, he was showing the right way to handle conflict; it's unreasonable to think Christians won't have conflicts like everyone else.)*

● **Why is it especially important for Christians to fight fair?** *(We need to show love, even in our conflicts; if we don't fight fair, we'll lose our credibility.)*

Say: **If we remember to avoid what's on these Foul Cards, we'll go a long way toward learning to handle conflicts with our friends in the right way.**

Unfair Fighting

Photocopy and cut apart the following cards.

FOUL CARD 1

Scorekeeping—During a *current* argument or discussion, you bring up instances of your friend's *past* failures or wrongdoings. This keeps the focus off the problem at hand.

Loose-Lips Card A

Late again? You're *always* late! I've *never* seen you get to anything before it starts. You know, *everybody* says that about you. This is impossible!

FOUL CARD 2

Character Bombing—Instead of dealing with the conflict, issue, or problem to be solved, you attack the other person's character or personality.

Loose-Lips Card B

Oh yeah? Remember the time you borrowed my basketball and put a hole in it? And what about all those times you lost things I loaned you? Just last week you busted my bike chain. I'm not even going to mention that little incident four years ago—you know what I'm talking about...

FOUL CARD 3

Piling On—You think of all the "bad" things your friend *has* done, *is* doing, or *will* do, and you just overwhelm him or her with it. It's like football players gang-tackling. Your friend has little chance to recover from this nonstop verbal dumping.

Loose-Lips Card C

I'm tired of you forgetting about me, like just now making me wait for you. And yesterday you didn't call until nine o'clock. You'll probably be busy all weekend and leave me by myself, just like you forgot about my birthday. And hey, what about your promise to help me with my math? And another thing...

FOUL CARD 4

Generalizing—Instead of being specific, you use words like "always," "never," and "every time." You move from dealing with a particular problem to making a big deal out of *everything*.

Loose-Lips Card D

Well, all I can say is that maybe you disappointed me a little. And don't ask me to explain, because I think you know what I mean. And if you don't, you should. Besides, I'm not so sure I would want a friend who couldn't understand what's upsetting me...

FOUL CARD 5

Fogging—You speak in such vague terms that you can't really be accused of attacking your friend. You *seem* to imply something is wrong, and your tone is rather threatening. This is the opposite of "speaking the truth in love."

Loose-Lips Card E

If only you weren't so selfish. You always want your own way. You're just about the most conceited, creepy sleazebag I've ever seen!

FOUL CARD 6

Counterattacking—Instead of really listening to a friend's complaints and responding to them, you make up your own complaints to sling right back. No communication really takes place—just a series of verbal attacks with pauses for reloading.

Loose-Lips Card F

So you think *I* ignored *you* at the party, huh? Well, I think *you* ignored *me* at the game.

Don't Say It

Purpose:

Students will explore how communication breaks down and examine ways to avoid miscommunication.

Supplies:

You'll need Bibles.

Experience:

Form groups of five or fewer. Have each group designate one person to act as the "Receiver." Send all the Receivers out of the room.

While the Receivers are gone, have groups each come up with three to five "actions" they'll get the Receiver to act out with them—without talking. Tell groups to make the actions wild and crazy, but identifiable. Explain that groups will have to get their Receivers to guess what actions they are acting out.

Offer suggestions to get groups thinking on the right track—for example, a group might act out eating a bologna sandwich while riding on the wing of an airplane or watching adventure movies while resting on the bottom of the ocean.

Tell students they can use their arms and legs and make any noise they want—even hum a tune—as long as they don't say any words. When groups are ready, call all the Receivers and explain to them what's expected of them. Allow groups to go one at a time, congratulating Receivers if they guess correctly.

After all the groups have had their fun, ask:

● **What did you enjoy about this activity?** *(Having people act out and guess goofy things; trying to communicate something very original without words.)*

● **What went through your mind as you tried to get your message across to your Receiver?** *(I was frustrated, I couldn't get the message across; I felt frustrated, the Receiver couldn't understand what my actions meant.)*

● **How did you feel as a Receiver?** *(Angry, they didn't act it out well enough that I could guess it; stupid, I couldn't understand what they were trying to get me to do.)*

● **How is this experience like communication breakdown in real life? How is it different? Explain.** *(It's unlike real life, it usually isn't this funny; it's just like real life, you feel frustrated because you're not being understood.)*

● **What should we do when communication breaks down?** *(Listen more carefully; talk it out as soon as possible.)*

Say: **In this game, misunderstandings created a lot of fun. But mis-understandings can lead to tough problems and wasted energy. Let's see how Jesus handled some of the misunderstandings he faced.**

Form two groups, and assign each group one of these passages to present as a skit: Matthew 16:5-12 or John 3:1-7. Have each group create its skit and present it to the other group. Then ask each group:

● **What was the misunderstanding in your passage?** *(The disciples didn't understand Jesus was talking about the Pharisees' and Saducees' teachings, not about bread; Nicodemus thought Jesus was telling him he had to go back to his mother's womb in order to get to heaven.)*

● **What negative results could have come from this communication breakdown?** *(The disciples wouldn't have understood Jesus' warning about the Pharisees and Saducees; Nicodemus wouldn't have understood how to enter God's kingdom.)*

● **How did Jesus prevent those negative results?** *(He told the disci-ples they had misunderstood him; he further explained to Nicodemus what he meant by "born again.")*

● **What lessons can we learn from Jesus about handling communi-cation breakdowns?** *(Question others when you think they're misunderstanding you; be sensitive to what other people are hearing, not just what you're saying.)*

Say: **There are lots of good ways to avoid a communication break-down—saying what you mean in more than one way, asking questions, even asking the other person to repeat what you said. But when com-munication breakdowns do happen, we should deal with them as soon as possible. That way we can avoid problems for ourselves and others.**

Exercising Rights

Purpose:

Students will explore what the Bible says about rights and privileges.

Supplies:

You'll need Bibles, masking tape, cookies, napkins, punch, cups, a tape player and a cassette or a compact disc player and a CD, chairs, paper, pencils, scissors, and the "My Rights" handout (p. 38).

Experience:

With masking tape, make two lines on the floor that intersect in the center, dividing the room into four quadrants. Designate each quadrant as A, B, C, or D. Put cookies and napkins in Quadrant A; punch and cups in Quadrant B; a tape player and a cassette or a compact disc player and a CD in Quadrant C; and chairs in Quadrant D.

Form four groups, and put a different group in each quadrant. (A group can be one person.) Give groups each the appropriate "My Rights" handout section (p. 38).

Say: **For the next six minutes, you have only the rights listed on your card. Don't worry about other groups' rights—just exercise your own. Follow the rules on your handout, and do your best to enjoy some cookies, punch, and music during this time.**

Give groups six minutes to exercise their rights—or protest the lack of certain rights. If groups try to exercise rights they don't have, tell the whole group what they're doing and take away more of that group's rights for "breaking the law."

After six minutes, have groups sit in their own quadrants. Ask:

● **What did you think about your rights?** (*I didn't like our group's rights; we didn't have enough rights; we had plenty of rights.*)

● **How did you feel when you had a right but you couldn't exercise it? Explain.** (*Frustrated, I wanted to have some punch but I couldn't cross the line to get it; fine, I had the right to play loud music but I didn't care to.*)

● **How did you feel when your rights clashed with someone else's? Explain.** (*Angry, I wanted to exercise my right of peace and quiet but another group was playing loud music; it was fun, I enjoy the challenge of clashing with someone else.*)

● **Were you tempted to cheat and exercise a right you didn't have? Why or why not?** *(Yes, I didn't think it was fair that other people could have food and punch; no, I followed the rules even though I wished I'd had more rights.)*

Give cookies and punch to the groups that didn't already have some. Continue the discussion by asking:

● **How was this activity like what happens with rights in the real world?** *(Some people seem to have more rights than others; people's rights often clash.)*

Have students describe situations that are similar to the ones students experienced in this activity—for example, they may say, "Homeless people don't seem to have the right to shelter" or "Rich people sometimes overrule the rights of poor people." Ask:

● **What's our responsibility as Christians when it comes to people's rights?** *(We should stand up for our rights; we should help people who don't have as many rights; we should give up our rights when they clash with others' rights.)*

● **Are the rights we've been talking about really more like privileges? Why or why not?** *(Yes, we've been given the opportunities for freedom of speech and other freedoms, not because we deserve them but as a gift; no, we really deserve these rights.)*

Say: **Until now, we've been talking about personal rights. Yet maybe we should think about these rights as privileges. We don't have rights because we deserve them, but because God has granted them to us. Let's look at what the Bible has to say about rights.**

Have students remain in their quadrant groups. Read aloud Exodus 22:21-27; Matthew 5:38-42; and Philippians 2:3-5. Ask:

● **What do these verses tell us about rights?** *(We need to give up our rights sometimes; we need to think of others' needs before our own; God will defend our rights.)*

● **According to these verses, why is it sometimes important to give up a right or privilege?** *(Because others' needs are more important; because we're supposed to be humble.)*

● **Is it easy to give up a privilege you have? Why or why not?** *(No, I like having certain freedoms and I would miss them; yes, if God wants me to give up a privilege, I'll gladly do it.)*

Give groups each a sheet of paper and a pencil. Have groups each discuss which right on their "My Rights" handout section from the previous activity they'd be willing to give to another group. Then have them decide which group they'd give the right to. Have them each write it on paper. For example, the group in Quadrant D might decide to give the right to sit in chairs to the group in Quadrant C.

Have groups each present their papers to the appropriate group. Then have groups act out their new rights for a minute or two. Ask:

● **How difficult was it to give up your rights?** *(Very difficult, we didn't have many to begin with; easy, others needed this right more than we did.)*

● **How is giving up one of your rights in this activity like following the principles outlined in the Bible verses?** *(We had to think of others' needs ahead of ours; it's different, we gave what we didn't need instead of what others needed.)*

● **When should we yield our rights to others?** *(When we're simply being stubborn about our rights; when holding on to our rights hurts others.)*

Remove the tape that separated the quadrants. Have students go around and shake hands with each other. Then have students form a circle.

Say: **The Bible gives us clear messages concerning rights. It tells us God will defend our rights. And it tells us we may have to give up rights from time to time, and that we should look out for others' rights. How we respond to these messages is what's most important.**

MY RIGHTS

Photocopy this handout, and cut apart the sections. Give one section to each group.

MY RIGHTS—Group A

You have:
- the right to eat.
- the right to enjoy peace and quiet.
- the right to cross into other quadrants.

You don't have:
- the right to play loud music.
- the right to drink punch.
- the right to sit in chairs.
- the right to protest your situation.

MY RIGHTS—Group B

You have:
- the right to eat.
- the right to enjoy peace and quiet.
- the right to cross into other quadrants.
- the right to drink punch.
- the right to protest your situation.

You don't have:
- the right to sit in chairs.
- the right to play loud music.

MY RIGHTS—Group C

You have:
- the right to play loud music.
- the right to eat.
- the right to protest your situation.

You don't have:
- the right to sit in chairs.
- the right to cross into other quadrants.
- the right to drink punch.

MY RIGHTS—Group D

You have:
- the right to drink punch.
- the right to sit in chairs.
- the right to play loud music.

You don't have:
- the right to cross into other quadrants.
- the right to eat.
- the right to protest your situation.

Feats of Clay

Purpose:

Students will explore the qualities of a perfect friend.

Supplies:

You'll need Bibles, modeling clay (in five different colors), pencils, and one copy of the "Quality Check" handout (p. 41) for each person.

Experience:

Form groups of no more than four, and give each group five portions of modeling clay (one portion each of five different colors). (If you don't have clay, you can use different-colored construction paper instead.) Have group members work together to choose the five most important qualities of a good friend. When the groups have chosen five qualities, have them each assign one quality to each color of clay.

Say: **I want you to sculpt the perfect friend, using each color of clay to the degree you want that quality in your friend. For example, if honesty is very important to you and you've assigned the red clay to represent that quality, then you would sculpt a friend made up of mostly red clay.**

Allow groups about three minutes to discuss how they'll create their friends and to sculpt their friends. When groups are finished, have volunteers from each group explain their sculptures. Then ask:

● **What went through your mind as you created your perfect friend?** *(It helped me to see what I really want in a friend; I was wondering if I'll ever find a friend like the one I created.)*

● **How similar is your "ideal friend" to what you're like with your friends? Explain.** *(Pretty similar, but I'm not that loyal; not very similar, I think I have different friendship qualities.)*

● **How is your ideal friend like your real friends?** *(Real friends aren't always so consistent; even my friends have qualities that bother me.)*

● **What could you do to become more like your ideal friend?** *(I could try to be more understanding when my friends have problems; I could stop cutting down my friends so much.)*

Say: **We've all heard the phrase, "You've got to be a friend to get a friend." That's really true. As you work at becoming the kind of friend** you want for yourself, you'll find new friends with the qualities you're looking for.

Ask for volunteers to read aloud Proverbs 17:17 and John 15:13. Ask:

● **What qualities do these verses say are important in a good friend?** *(Friends stick by you; they help you when you're in trouble; they're friends even if others don't like you; they put your feelings before their feelings; they lay themselves down for you.)*

● **How do these qualities compare with the qualities you felt were important?** *(They're the same ones we had on our list; they're similar to mine; I think our list is better.)*

● **How do you compare with the qualities listed in these verses?** *(I have a long way to go before I'm that good a friend; I think I do what those verses say most of the time.)*

Pass out the "Quality Check" handouts (p. 41) and pencils. Give students each a few minutes to rate themselves on how they'd react to the situations on the handout. When students are finished, form pairs. Have partners tell each other about one real-life situation in which a friend responded to them in a way that was really loving.

Read aloud the verses again. Then have each student tell his or her partner one way the partner is the kind of friend these verses describe.

Say: **All of us have some of the qualities that make for super friendships, but there are always ways we can each become more like the kind of friends God wants us to be.**

Quality Check

Rate yourself! How do you think you'd react to these situations? Read each entry, and put a check next to the response that best describes how closely your reaction would be to what's written. Be honest!

Allie had hurt Meg's feelings badly, but she wanted to make things right. She approached Meg at school the day after their fight and said she was sorry. Meg responded, "That's nice, but I'm just not ready to forgive you." Would you respond like Meg?
I'd respond like Meg:

Always   **Sometimes**   **Never!**

Ned knew Gregory from church. He didn't mind hanging out with Gregory at church, but at school, Gregory was, well, a lot different than the other students. One day Gregory caught sight of Ned in the hall and tried to give him the "Jesus Jab" handshake they'd made up at church. Ned ignored him and walked on. Would you have done the same?
I'd respond like Ned:

Always   **Sometimes**   **Never!**

Sarah and Kyle had grown up next door to each other, but they'd gone in different directions as they grew older. The night Sarah's dad died, Kyle sat up with Sarah and her family even though it meant he'd miss the team bus to the basketball final. Would you make the same choice?
I'd respond like Kyle:

Always   **Sometimes**   **Never!**

Find a New Way

Purpose:

Students will discover new ways to show love to their parents.

Supplies:

You'll need Bibles, index cards, pencils, tape, newsprint, and markers.

Experience:

Say: **Talking to parents can be tough. It's hard to open up, and it isn't always easy to get your point across.**

Form pairs. Designate one partner in each pair as Siskel and the other as Ebert. Send the Siskels and the Eberts to opposite ends of the room to receive their instructions. Give the Siskels each an index card and a pencil.

Say: **Write a positive, honest message about your partner, such as "You're very giving" or "I like the way you smile." In a few minutes, you'll give it to your partner.**

While the Siskels are writing, go to the Eberts and say: **In a few minutes, your partner will come and give you a message. You must sit here and keep your eyes closed. Don't peek.**

Return to the Siskels, and say: **Take your message to your partner now. You may not talk at all.**

As the Siskels deliver their messages, have the Eberts keep their eyes closed. Ask:

● **What's the problem here?** *(They're not getting the message; what's this card for?)*

● **What were you thinking as you were trying to give or receive the message?** *(I was frustrated; I wanted to see what my partner had written.)*

To the Siskels, say: **Find another way to give your message to your partner. You can speak, but the Eberts still can't see.**

After the messages are delivered, ask:

● **How do you feel now that you gave or received the message completely?** *(Relieved; surprised at the message.)*

Say: **There are different ways to express love and thanks. Sometimes we get into a rut and only do it one way. Today we'll discover new ways to express love to our parents. Let's start by looking at biblical examples** of expressing love.

Tape a sheet of newsprint to the wall. On the newsprint, write the words to John 15:12. Leave space to write under the verse. Set a few markers near the newsprint.

Say: **Before Jesus died on the cross, he met with his disciples one last time to tell them what would happen and to give them instructions. One command he gave is, "Love each other as I have loved you." Let's look at some verses to find out different ways Jesus showed his love.**

Form groups of three, and give each student a Bible. Assign groups each one of the following passages. Have groups read their passages and then write on the newsprint ways Jesus shows love in that Scripture. If you have fewer than six groups, have some groups look up two passages. If you have more than six groups, assign the same passage to multiple groups.

● Matthew 8:2-3 (Jesus gets involved—he touches the man and heals him.)

● Matthew 20:29-34 (Jesus asks, "What do you want me to do for you?" and takes a personal interest in the men.)

● Luke 22:32 (Jesus prays for Peter.)

● Luke 23:33-34 (Jesus died on the cross, asking God to forgive people.)

● John 13:3-5 (Jesus washed his disciples' feet.)

● John 3:16 (Jesus died in our place.)

Ask:

● **How do these verses relate to the communication game we played earlier?** *(There are many different ways to show love; sometimes it's hard to show love no matter how you try to do it.)*

● **How many ways are there to show love?** *(An infinite number; too many to count.)*

● **How would your life be different if you loved others the same way Jesus did?** *(I'd be very popular; I'd feel good about myself.)*

Say: **Jesus showed his love in practical, everyday ways. He was faithful, he listened to people, and he met their needs. Jesus commands us to love others the way he loves us.** Ask:

● **How could you express Jesus' kind of love in the following situations?**

1. You're watching your favorite TV show. Your mom comes home with a car full of groceries and has brought in two bags. *(Help carry bags in; help unpack groceries; thank Mom for shopping; offer to put food away after the show is over.)*

2. Your dad's been out of town for several days and is coming home tonight. It's been snowing all day. *(Shovel the sidewalk; make him a treat; make a welcome-home banner.)*

3. Your mom's been really tired and not feeling well the past few days. *(Ask her how she's feeling; offer to make supper or do the laundry; ask how you can help.)*

4. Your mom's driven you to three activities this week so far. *(Thank her; make her a card thanking her; offer to help her with something at home.)*

5. Your dad's been working overtime all week and comes home exhausted and crabby. *(Thank him for working; serve him a treat; put on music he likes.)*

6. You want to wear certain clothes for a special event at school tomorrow but they need to be washed. *(Offer to fix supper so Mom can start the laundry; start the laundry and see if Mom needs anything washed; tell her about your special event and ask for her help; wear something else.)*

After students have responded, ask:

● **How would your parents feel if you did any of these things?** *(Shocked; loved.)*

● **How do your parents know you love them?** *(They just do; by how I treat them.)*

Say: **It's not always easy to say "I love you" to your parents. But it's extremely important to let them know how you feel. During the coming week, come up with as many new ways to show love to your parents as you can. Then try out those ideas. You'll be amazed at how powerful such a positive message can be.**

From Where I Am

Purpose:

Students will discover that by working together, they can make lasting changes in people's lives.

Supplies:

You'll need a Bible, balloons, markers, tape, and paper in two different colors.

Experience:

Have students stand, spacing themselves evenly around the room. Give each person two or three balloons and a marker. Ask students to brainstorm about different needs or problems they know exist in your town—some examples are crime, violence, abuse, alcoholism, loneliness, drug abuse, truancy, homelessness, poverty, teen pregnancy, AIDS, or cancer. Have students each inflate their balloons, tie them off, and write a different one of the needs or problems on each balloon.

Tell students to drop their balloons on the floor and kick them away. Say: **On "go," I want you to pop as many balloons as you can with your right foot. Your left foot must not move from the spot it's now in. If you can't reach a balloon, kick it to someone else to pop. Ready? Go!**

When students have popped as many balloons as they can, ask:

● **How did it feel to pop the balloons?** *(It was fun; I was frustrated because I couldn't reach all the balloons I wanted to pop.)*

● **Are you surprised at how many balloons you could pop without moving far? Why or why not?** *(Yes, we popped all the balloons without having to move; no, I knew we could do it if we worked together.)*

● **How is popping the balloons like tackling local problems as Christians?** *(It's easier than we might think; we only have to do what's within our reach to accomplish.)*

● **How is kicking the balloons to each other like working together as the church?** *(We can't do it all by ourselves, but by working together we can really make a difference; we had to cooperate with each other and not just worry about popping the balloons ourselves.)*

Say: **It's easy to think of problems as being too big or too far away. But there are needs in our own city that we can each help to meet. And by working together, we can create a lasting change in people's lives.**

Let's see what kind of impact we're making now in others' lives and compare our lifestyles to God's standard in Scripture.

Give students each some tape. On opposite sides of the room, lay out two different colors of paper. Label one "sheep" and the other "goats."

Read aloud Matthew 25:31-46. Say: **This passage shows us just how important God considers putting faith into action. We must remember that we're saved by faith alone, but true faith is always expressed through actions.**

I'll ask a series of questions about ways you may put your own faith into action. After each question, go to the "sheep" side of the room if you answer yes and the "goat" side if you answer no. Each time you do this, tear off a strip of the colored paper there and tape it to your shirt.

Note: The point of this exercise is to encourage students in the ways they already show their faith and to make them aware of more ways they might live out God's love in their lives. Be sure to ask questions that you know will get both yes and no answers from the students. Here are some suggestions:

- **Have you ever visited someone who was in prison?**
- **Have you ever visited someone in the hospital?**
- **Have you ever donated used clothes?**
- **Have you ever seen someone who needed some article of clothing and given yours to him or her?**
- **Have you ever introduced yourself to a stranger?**
- **Have you ever provided food for someone who was hungry?**
- **Have you ever given a drink to someone who was thirsty?**
- **Have you ever spent time with someone who was sick and homebound?**
- **Have you ever taken someone into your home because he or she had nowhere else to go?**
- **Do you pray for others?**

When students have collected several strips of each color, gather everyone together and ask:

- **How did it feel to get a "sheep" strip?** *(Good; it made me realize how much I already do for God.)*
- **How did it feel to get a "goat" strip?** *(Embarrassing; I wanted to do better.)*
- **What are other ways you try to make a difference in your community?** *(Volunteer somewhere; offer to baby-sit for a poor family.)*

Form a circle, and give students each a sheep strip and a piece of tape. One at a time, have students each tell one way the person across from him or her in the circle lives like a sheep in God's flock at home. Then have the students tape their sheep strips to the people across from them. Make sure each person receives only one sheep strip so that everyone will get one.

Say: **With God's help, even our smallest efforts can make a difference in our great big world.**

Hand-to-Hand Combat

Purpose:

Students will explore how to make choices that can diffuse even the most volatile situations.

Supplies:

You'll need Bibles.

Experience:

Form pairs, and have partners stand about six inches apart with their feet spread and their hands shoulder-high with the palms forward. Tell students that the goal of this "experiment" is for them to knock their partners off balance without losing their own balance in the process. Tell students they can touch only their partners' hands. Their hands must remain open—no gripping—and their feet may not move.

Allow students to do the experiment for several minutes. Every few minutes, tell students to switch partners and start again.

After several minutes, ask:

● **What were your thoughts during this experiment?** *(I felt confident, it was fun; I was frustrated, my partner pushed too hard.)*

● **How is this experiment similar to conflict in your personal life?** *(I wanted control of the situation; I fought to get the upper hand.)*

● **If slapping each other's hands represents conflict, what physical actions might represent ways to deal effectively with conflict?** *(Hugging each other; shaking hands.)*

● **What are effective ways to handle conflict that's caused by ineffective communication?** *(Talk as soon as possible, but not while you're angry; listen to the other person rather than fighting for your own position.)*

● **What are examples of wrong ways to handle conflict caused by ineffective communication?** *(Talk about the other person behind his or her back; stop talking to that person.)*

Say: **Conflicts don't always have to be like the game we just played. Rather than going head-to-head or hand-to-hand against someone, we** can make choices that can diffuse even the most volatile situations.

Form groups of four, and assign each group one of these two passages: Luke 4:16-30 or Acts 26:24-31. It's OK if more than one group has the same Bible passage. Tell each group it has seven minutes to create a dramatization of its passage, putting special emphasis on the conflicts described there.

After seven minutes, have each group present its dramatization. Applaud each group's efforts.

Then ask:

● **How would you have handled these situations?** *(I would have yelled at Festus; I would have run away.)*

● **How did Paul and Jesus deal with the conflicts they faced?** *(Jesus left; Paul answered with kindness and humor.)*

● **What other effective ways might Jesus and Paul have used?** *(There was no other way for Jesus to deal with the situation; Paul could have ignored Festus and just continued talking to Agrippa.)*

Say: **Conflict is not fun, but we can actually turn conflict around for good by applying the tips we've discussed today in handling volatile situations.**

How Firm Is Your Foundation?

Purpose:

Students will explore the importance of a solid faith foundation when reaching out to others.

Supplies:

You'll need Bibles, building blocks, paper, and pencils.

Experience:

Give each of the students twenty building blocks. If you don't have enough blocks for everyone in your group, use fist-sized rocks, books, or shoes instead. Tell students they're going to build pyramids that reflect how they live out their faith.

Ask the "Pyramid Questions" in sets as indicated (see page 51). The first set represents the foundation of the pyramid. For each question students answer "yes" to in the first set, have them add one block to their foundations. The next set represents the next level of the pyramid, and so on. For every question students can answer "yes" to, have them add a block to their pyramids at the appropriate level. Remind students to stick to the guidelines even if their pyramids can't stand up or don't look like pyramids.

When students have finished their pyramids, note how they are shaped. Ask:

● **What went through your mind as you built your pyramid?** *(I was a little concerned because I didn't know if my pyramid would stand; I was excited to see how it turned out.)*

● **Are your creations stable? Why or why not?** *(Yes, because I was able to build a large foundation; no, mine's top-heavy because my base is small.)*

● **What do our pyramids say about our faith?** *(It's easier to do the more superficial things; it's important to have a good foundation.)*

Say: **In the Christian life, everything is built on the foundation of our personal relationship with Jesus. Without a good foundation of personal faith in Christ, our lives can become unbalanced and shaky. But with a good foundation, God gives us the desire to reach out to the world around us and make a difference.**

Pyramid Questions

SET 1

1. Do you pray daily?
2. Do you worship with other Christians and learn about the Christian faith at least four times a month?
3. Have you ever volunteered at a food pantry, homeless shelter, or another place where people's physical needs are met?
4. Have you seen a person in *any* kind of need and taken immediate action to meet that need?
5. Have you spoken to someone about your relationship with Jesus in the past week?

SET 2

1. Have you told at least one family member you love him or her in the past week?
2. Have you ever done something you really didn't want to do because of your faith in Jesus?
3. Have you searched through the Bible for answers to a particular question or problem?
4. Have you given time or money to help someone in need within the past month?

SET 3

1. Have you ever refused to listen to or pass on a piece of gossip?
2. Did you control your temper when you wanted to lash out with words or actions during the past few weeks?
3. Have you ever told someone that God loves him or her?
4. Have you done work around the house recently before your parents asked you to?

SET 4

1. Have you ever hugged someone just because you love him or her?
2. Have you ever done something nice for someone, knowing you would receive no thanks?
3. Have you done something your parents asked you to do in the past week?

SET 5

1. Did you smile at someone who looked in need of a smile this week?
2. Did you tell someone you appreciate him or her in the past week?

Ask:

● **What things can you do in your own life to make your foundation more stable?** *(Have a consistent time alone with God each day; read my Bible more often.)*

Form two groups. Give each person in one group paper and a pencil. Don't give anything to the other group. Say nothing, but proceed with the lesson. If students ask about the paper and pencils, tell them that they're gifts and those who have them can do as they please with them.

Assign each group one of these two passages: Isaiah 61:1-3 and James 2:14-17. Say: **In the last activity, we talked about things that help us build a firm foundation as Christians. But once the foundation is laid, just what is God looking for from us? Use your assigned passage to find out. Read the passage, and summarize on paper what God wants from us.**

Watch what students do with the paper and pencils. Eventually, some students will tear their papers in two and share their pencils so the other group can do the activity.

When everyone is ready, have groups share their answers. Then ask the group that had no paper:

● **How did it feel to not have all you needed to do the activity?** *(I felt frustrated; I felt angry.)*

● **How is that like the way people who don't have a relationship with Jesus feel when they try to tackle life?** *(Life can be overwhelming for them; they try really hard to be happy, but there's always something missing.)*

Ask the group who had the paper:

● **How did it feel to watch the other group struggle to do the activity without paper?** *(I felt sorry for them; I wanted to give them my paper.)*

● **What did you do to respond to their need?** *(I ripped my paper in two; I didn't do anything.)*

● **How is that like the way we reach out to the world around us to make a difference?** *(We have to make a sacrifice to help others; we sometimes don't try to help even when we know we could.)*

Say: **Before we should try to make a difference in the world around us, we have to develop our own compassion and concern for people around us. It's not enough just to know it's the right thing to do. We need to do it for the right reasons, too.**

Human Towers

Purpose:

Students will explore how cooperation makes everyone a winner.

Supplies:

You'll need Bibles, tape, newsprint, and markers.

Experience:

Form groups of five or six, and have students in each group build a tower out of their bodies. (You may have to go outside if your ceiling is low.)

Tell the groups to make their towers as high as they can and stable enough to stand for thirty seconds. Be careful not to suggest any competition or comparison between the groups.

While the groups are building, listen for cooperative and competitive statements. When all the groups have finished their towers, congratulate each group's efforts. Ask:

● **How does cooperation help us to accomplish tasks?** *(We can accomplish lots of things together that we can't do alone; we can learn from each other if we cooperate.)*

● **Did you feel like you were competing with the other groups while you built your tower? Why or why not?** *(No, you didn't say it was a contest; yes, I just assumed we were.)*

● **How is assuming we were competing like what happens in real life sometimes?** *(When someone looks at you, it's easy to think they're comparing you to themselves; it's easy to think we're competing against others even when we really aren't.)*

● **What do people gain from cooperation?** *(When we work together, we all win; when we work as a team, no one has to be left out or feel like a loser.)*

● **How can we apply this experience to the way we handle competition and cooperation in our youth group?** *(We should work together rather than putting each other down; we can try to help each other rather than just looking out for ourselves.)*

Say: **Competition can sometimes be good because it keeps us pressing on to improve ourselves. But cooperating is always good, because when we work together, everyone always comes out a winner.**

Form two groups. Have one group read Galatians 5:13-15. Tape a sheet of newsprint to the wall. Provide markers, and have students in that group work together to create a symbol that represents the Scripture passage. It's OK if the symbol has many parts, but it must be one symbol.

Have the other group read Ecclesiastes 4:9-12 and work together to create a human sculpture that represents the Scripture passage. The only rule is that every member of the group must be a part of the sculpture.

When groups are ready, have each group explain its symbol or sculpture. Read aloud both Scriptures and then ask:

● **What do these Scriptures have to say about cooperation versus competition?** *(Cooperation is better because you can do more; competition can lead to hate and destruction.)*

● **How was working on the symbol or creating the sculpture an example of the kind of cooperation these passages talk about?** *(We had to work together to come up with one symbol we all liked; the sculpture we created required every person to play a part.)*

● **How can we keep this kind of cooperation even when we're competing in sports or something similar?** *(By remembering that loving others is more important than winning; by wanting the best for others even if that means you don't win.)*

Say: **By working together, we can do much more than we could ever do alone.**

Is That What I Said?

Purpose:

Students will explore ways good communication can help resolve family conflicts.

Supplies:

You'll need Bibles, one "Draw This" handout (p. 58) for each pair, pencils, paper, one "War Zone" handout (p. 59) for each person, newsprint, a marker, and tape.

Experience:

Have students form pairs and sit back-to-back on the floor, allowing plenty of space between pairs. Give one partner in each pair a copy of the "Draw This" handout (p. 58), and give the other partner in each pair a pencil and a sheet of paper.

Say: **Those of you who have the "Draw This" handout are to give your partners verbal instructions that will help them reproduce on their papers the picture you're looking at. You have two minutes to create your masterpieces. Go!**

Call time after two minutes, and have pairs compare the pictures they created to the "Draw This" handout. Give a hearty round of applause to each of the artists. Then ask:

● **Was this activity difficult? Why or why not?** *(Yes, it was hard to tell exactly what I was supposed to draw; yes, it was difficult to give clear directions.)*

● **What does this show you about communication?** *(It's not easy to say what you mean; people can take the things you say in different ways.)*

● **How is this lack of clear communication like what sometimes happens in families?** *(People don't always understand things the way you mean them.)*

Say: **When conflict is in the air and emotions are running high, we really need to "listen between the lines." I'll give you some examples. You listen between the lines and tell me what I might really be saying.** Read the following sentences, and have students guess the responses.

● **Just leave me alone.** *(I'm having a really bad day.)*

● **You idiot!** *(I'm totally frustrated, and I'm turning my frustration on you.)*

● **I don't have to listen to this.** *(It would be more constructive to talk about this another time.)*

● **You always do this to me!** *(This is a problem we've had before, and we need to find a solution.)*

● **I can't believe how stupid I am.** *(I'm disappointed with myself and I don't know how anyone could like me.)*

Say: **Listening between the lines is one of the skills that will help us learn how to work through conflicts. Now let's listen between the lines of a very famous argument between sisters.**

Have students look up Luke 10:38-42. Ask a volunteer to read the passage aloud. Then ask:

● **Whose side are you on in this conflict? Explain.** *(Martha's, I don't think she should have to do all the work; Mary's, she knew what was most important.)*

● **How do you feel about the answer Jesus gave?** *(He showed that he cared for Martha by the way he said her name; I don't understand why he didn't make Mary help.)*

● **Is asking someone you respect to be a mediator a legitimate way to settle a conflict?** *(Yes, because you get an objective opinion; no, it's like telling on someone.)*

Say: **Mary and Martha's home was suddenly full of visitors— important visitors. That's enough to add stress to any family! Let's find out what kinds of situations can turn your house into a war zone.**

Distribute the "War Zone" handout (p. 59). Give students a couple of minutes to rate their top five conflict points. Then tally the number of students who checked each item to discover the top conflict points for your youth group.

Say: **Now that we know what our hot topics are, let's figure out what to do about them. Find a different partner and share your answers to these questions.**

● **Of the hot topics you checked, which can you take personal responsibility for?**

● **What action can you take to keep these conflicts from recurring?**

● **How do you feel about the way your parents handle these conflicts? What do you wish they'd do differently?**

Say: **Let's turn our attention to some techniques you can use to resolve these conflicts. Our first one comes from Jesus himself.**

Have a volunteer read aloud Matthew 18:15-16. Then ask:

● **What do you think about this advice from Jesus?** *(You have to be brave to do that; most people don't want to hear what they've done wrong; you* *need to be careful how you approach the person.)*

Say: **When you're trying to settle a conflict, timing and attitude are everything. Here are some simple guidelines.** Write these points on a sheet of newsprint or a chalkboard:

- Take time out.
- Put yourself in the other person's shoes.
- Listen.
- Learn to say, "I'm sorry."

Say: **Now let's go through these points; I'd like you to tell me why each one is important.** Ask:

- **What's the point of taking a timeout?** *(You get perspective on the situation; you get rid of the adrenaline rush and think more clearly; if you keep talking when you're mad, you end up saying things you don't really mean.)*
- **Why is it important to put yourself in the other person's shoes?** *(Because every story has two sides; you need to realize how your actions affect other people.)*
- **How can you let people know you're really listening?** *(By looking them in the eye and nodding your head; by rephrasing what they say and asking if that's correct.)*
- **Why is listening so important?** *(It shows respect for the other person's point of view; if you listen to the other person, he or she will be more inclined to listen to you.)*
- **What are the hardest words to say in any language?** *(I'm sorry.)*
- **Why is saying them so important?** *(Because it's healthy to accept responsibility for our mistakes; because it opens the way toward resolution and healing.)*

Say: **One last thing—it's important to realize that you can't change anyone else's behavior. You can only change your own behavior and your own reactions. These aren't simple solutions that will suddenly make everything OK in your life. But they're important tools you can use to resolve conflict in a Christlike way.**

Draw This

War Zone

Which of these issues can turn your house into a war zone? Rate your top five conflict points, with one being the top conflict point.

___messy room   ___your choice of friends

___coming home too late   ___spending money

___home responsibilities   ___church attendance

___bad language   ___performance in school

___use of the phone   ___what you wear

___how you wear your hair

___choice of movies and TV programs

___use of the car

___other (write it here)_____

Lean on Me

Purpose:
Students will learn how mutual support, cooperation, and trust help build a foundation for a strong marriage.

Supplies:
You'll need Bibles, pencils, index cards, newsprint, markers, masking tape, and a copy of the "What Some Might Say" handout (p. 63).

Experience:

Form pairs. If there's an extra group member, become that student's partner and play along.

Have students in each pair introduce themselves to each other and shake hands. Then have them sit back-to-back on the floor and link elbows. On the count of three, have pairs try to stand up. Watch how partners work together—or fail to! Have pairs do this exercise a few times to see if they can improve their techniques. Then ask:

● **What were your feelings during this experience?** *(I felt stupid, we couldn't get up; it was great, we really worked together.)*

● **How is this like a friendship?** *(We had to work together; we needed to lean on each other for support.)*

● **How is this like a marriage?** *(Both people need to cooperate to make it work; it's not always easy to be connected to another person.)*

Comment on what you noticed during the game. For example, did you see some couples give up? Did some carefully plan their strategy before trying to stand? If so, draw parallels to how friendships and marriages operate.

Say: **Mutual support, cooperation, and trust are great qualities to have in a friend. And those friendship qualities help build a foundation for a strong marriage. Let's look at a Scripture passage that describes lasting friendship qualities and the kind of relationship you have with your best friend.**

Form groups no larger than five. Ask a volunteer to read aloud Colossians 3:12-14. Encourage students to follow along in their Bibles.

Hand out pencils and index cards—enough cards so each student has a card to represent each other student in his or her group.

Say: **Colossians says you must "clothe yourselves" with certain** qualities. We're going to "clothe" each other in a moment. Each of you has one index card for each person in your group. Please write on each card a friendship quality you see in one of the people in your group. For example, you could write that someone is kind or that someone else is a good listener. Continue until you've written a friendship quality for each person on a different card. Refer to Colossians 3:12-14 for ideas. Galatians 5:22-23 has good ideas, too.

While students are working, write the headings, "Good Friends" and "Marriage Qualities?" on separate sheets of newsprint. Under the heading "Marriage Qualities?" tape the "What Some Might Say" handout (p. 63).

Give each group some masking tape. Have students decide whose birthday is closest to today. That person will be the first to be clothed with friendship qualities. Have each group member tell what friendship quality describes that person and why and then tape the card to that person. When a group is finished with one person, have students in the group continue until each person is clothed in qualities.

After everyone is covered with cards, ask students to bring their qualities forward and tape them under the heading "Good Friends" on the newsprint. Suggest they group similar qualities together. For example, if there are four "good listener" cards, tell kids to clump them together.

Now read the "Marriages in Trouble" scenarios (p. 62) one by one. After each scenario, have students look at the two lists of qualities and ask:

● **Which, if any, of the traits on the "Marriage Qualities?" list would help the couple?** *(Probably none of those would help; they're more superficial traits.)*

Note: Students might joke, "Yeah, if Patty was good-looking, Andy wouldn't have run out on her." Bring the group around to a serious note by asking if they *really* think good looks or money would help in the long run. If the exercise works as planned, you'll find more helpful characteristics from Colossians and from what the students wrote under the "Good Friends" heading. Ask:

● **Which, if any, of the items on the "Good Friends" list would help the couple?** *(Loyal; trustworthy; is a good listener; helps with problems.)*

As students find "Good Friends" qualities that would help a couple, have someone tear the drawing of the couple from the "What Some Might Say" handout and tape it near those words.

After all the scenarios have been read, ask:

● **What did you discover about what makes a good marriage?** *(Qualities of a friend; characteristics God says you should clothe yourself with.)*

● **Why is friendship so vital to a marriage?** *(You can trust and depend on a friend; friends will stick by you no matter what.)*

● **What do you have to invest in a friendship to make it work?** *(Time; risks.)*

● **How is that like what two people invest in a marriage?** *(They need to spend time together; they need to communicate often.)*

Wrap up the discussion by asking a volunteer to read aloud Colossians 3:12-14.

Marriages in Trouble

Help! These couples are in trouble. What qualities do they need to mend their breaking relationships?

Couple 1—Andy finally admitted to Patty that he'd been cheating on her. All those times he said he was working late, he was really seeing another woman. What does this couple need?

Couple 2—Juanita and Joel never talk. It's just easier that way. It seems that whenever the two of them start discussing something, they end up fighting. What does this couple need?

Couple 3—Bev works a lot. She admits she's a workaholic. That means she always chooses work over time with Harvey. Harvey resents all the time Bev spends at her job. It's like they hardly know each other anymore. What does this couple need?

Couple 4—Wendy loves to talk. She's always got something she can't wait to tell Keith. But Keith comes home so bushed from working all day, he can't wait to relax and tune out the world. Wendy wants to talk, but Keith always wants it to wait. "I'm too tired, honey" or "Can't that wait until tomorrow?" are his favorite lines. Wendy's frustrated because tomorrow never comes. What does this couple need?

What Some Might Say

A national magazine asked teenagers which of these qualities were important to them in a relationship with the opposite sex. They listed these:

Good Personality   *Intelligence*   *Money*

Good Looks   *Sense of Humor*

Artistic Ability   *Sensitivity*

Andy and Patty

Juanita and Joel

Bev and Harvey

Keith and Wendy

The Longest Bridge

Purpose:
Students will explore why the way people compete is just as important as whether they win or lose.

Supplies:
You'll need Bibles; string, tape, craft sticks, and two boxes for each group of four or five; a book; and purple construction paper.

Experience:
Form groups of four or five. Give each group two boxes and an ample supply of string, tape, and craft sticks. Tell groups to compete to see which group can build the longest free-standing bridge.

Allow groups ten minutes to build their bridges. When the time is almost up and it's evident which group is going to win, pull aside a person from the winning group. Give him or her a book, and instruct him or her to go and drop the book on one of the losing groups' bridges.

Allow a few seconds for students to vent their emotions and then call everyone together. Ask the members of the "crushed" group:

● **How do you feel about your bridge being destroyed?** *(I'm really angry you let her destroy it; it wasn't fair; they were going to win anyway.)*

Ask the other groups:

● **What are your reactions to what happened?** *(I think the winning group should be disqualified; I don't think it's fair to the "crushed" group; I'm just glad they didn't destroy our bridge.)*

Ask the whole group:

● **How is this situation like what happens when people take competition too far?** *(It's not enough for some people to win, they have to hurt others in the process; some people make everybody hate them because they have such a bad attitude when they win at anything.)*

● **How does competition sometimes destroy the bridges, or relationships, between people?** *(Sometimes people put competition above* *friendship and that's not right; some people only care about themselves and they use their friends to help them win.)*

Say: **Winning really isn't everything. The way you compete is just as important as whether you win or lose. In fact, God thinks it's more important. Let's take a look at what the Bible has to say about the importance of love over winning.**

Give students each a sheet of purple construction paper. Say: **Tear a heart shape out of your construction paper. Then, as I read the following Scripture passage, I want you to tear off a piece of your heart every time you hear me mention any actions that would be hurtful in competition.**

Slowly read aloud Galatians 5:17-21, pausing to allow students to tear off pieces of their heart shapes whenever they hear actions that would be hurtful in competition.

After reading that passage, give students each several strips of tape, and say: **Now, as I read Galatians 5:22-23 and Colossians 3:12-17, I want you to reconstruct your heart with tape each time you hear an action or an attitude that would be good to have in competition.**

When the hearts are reconstructed, ask:

● **What went through your mind when you tore up your heart?** *(I understood better how hurtful competition can be; I felt sad.)*

● **What was it like to repair the damage done to the heart?** *(There were a lot more healing words than hurting words; even with all the tape, I couldn't make the heart like it was before.)*

● **How is the paper heart like a person's heart in a competitive situation?** *(People are more fragile than I thought, just like the paper; after you hurt someone, it's not the same for him or her even if you say you're sorry.)*

● **After hearing these passages, what do you think of the old adage, "It's not whether you win or lose, it's how you play the game"?** *(I think it's absolutely right, because winning isn't worth it when you hurt people; I agree, because the way you play is more important to God than whether you win or lose.)*

Say: **It takes more than winning to make a "winner." From God's perspective, the way you play is far more important than winning or losing.**

Munchie Mania

Purpose:
Students will explore the issue of hunger.

Supplies:
You'll need Bibles, a variety of unbreakable items, a bag of fun-size candy bars, a whistle, and pencils.

Experience:

Form two to four equal-sized teams of students. Line the teams up along different walls of the room. In the center of the room, put ten different unbreakable items such as a trash can, several Frisbees, a few balls, and a pillow. Assign one item a value of three thousand points, three items a value of one thousand points each, and six items a value of five hundred points each.

Show the teams a bag of fun-size candy bars. Advise the students that the object of this game is to gain enough points to "buy" the bag of candy bars for their teams.

Explain that you will call out one characteristic such as "people with green eyes" or "everyone wearing red" and then blow a whistle. When the whistle blows, those who match the characteristic called should try to grab as many of the items from the center of the room as possible and take them back to their teams' walls. Add up the point values for the items collected per team, and have teams return the items to the center. The first team to reach twenty thousand points can buy the candy bars.

Say: **There is one catch: inflation. Every two rounds, the cost of the candy bars goes up eight thousand points. Ready? Let's play!**

Play several rounds. See if any team is able to get enough points to buy the candy bars. Watch for the reactions of the team members each time you raise the price.

After the game, ask:

● **How might this game be like the way needy people face life?** (They try hard but they never have enough; they feel like giving up; they wonder if it will ever end.)

● **How did you feel each time the price of the candy bars went up?** (Like it was unfair; mad; like no one could get the candy bars.)

● **What would you do if your family suddenly found itself unable to buy food or pay for a place to live?** (Worry a lot; get a job; move in with my *grandparents; sell something.)*

● **How do you feel when you see people who are homeless or poor?** *(Like they should get a job; uncomfortable; sorry for them; I ignore them.)*

Form small groups of five or fewer, and distribute pencils and paper. Instruct each group to read Proverbs 21:13; Proverbs 22:16; and Matthew 25:31-46 and to summarize the theme of these Scriptures in their own words. Allow the groups to share. Ask:

● **Who does God seem to be concerned about in these Scriptures?** *(The poor; the hungry; strangers; the sick; prisoners.)*

● **Why do you think God feels so strongly about these people?** *(He loves them; he doesn't like to see them suffer.)*

● **How do your feelings about these people compare to God's feelings?** *(I'm not as concerned; these people scare me, but they don't scare God; I care like God cares.)*

Say: **People today often think only of their own needs, but the Bible clearly says we are to think of others. When we serve others, we also serve God.**

No Simple War

Purpose:

Students will explore why nations go to war.

Supplies:

You'll need Bibles, one copy of the "Pieces of the Pie" hand-out (p. 71), three copies of the "Pie Rules" handout (p. 72), scissors, dice, newsprint, a marker, tape, and three large marshmallows for each student.

Experience:

Form three equal-sized groups. (A group can be one person.) Give groups each a different "Why You Need the Pie" slip from the "Pieces of the Pie" handout (p. 71), four pie pieces from the "Pie Chart" on the same hand-out (randomly distributed), and a "Pie Rules" handout (p. 72).

Say: **Each group here represents a different country. You're all in-terested in taking control of a larger area of land surrounding your country. This land is represented by the pie pieces. The only way to get the land is to take it from the other groups. You each have differ-ent reasons for wanting the land, and you'll only win this game if you end up with seven pie pieces as outlined on your "Why You Need the Pie" slip. Read your slip and the "Pie Rules" handout in your groups. We'll start the game in a few minutes.**

Allow three or four minutes for groups to read their handouts and discuss their strategies for the game. Then give groups up to five minutes to play the game. Encourage groups to try different strategies to get seven pie pieces with the right symbols. If two groups declare war against each other, coordi-nate the war progress according to the rules on the "Pie Rules" handout.

Call time after five minutes or when all but one of the groups have been defeated in war or only one group has pie pieces left. Form a circle, and ask:

● **What was it like trying to get the pie pieces you wanted?** *(I was upset, no one would trade with us; I was frustrated.)*

● **How is that like the way two nations might feel if they were trying to claim ownership of the same piece of land or property?** *(They both might think they deserve to own the property; they both might feel angry or upset.)*

● **What prompted (or could have prompted) groups to go to war in this activity?** *(We all wanted the same pie pieces; we were afraid someone else would get all the pie pieces.)*

● **How are these reasons like the reasons nations go to war?** *(Nations fight over property; nations fight to keep others from getting too powerful.)*

● **Based on this exercise, are the reasons for going to war always simple? Explain.** *(No, people have different reasons for going to war; yes, war is always a selfish option.)*

Have students brainstorm reasons nations go to war. List these reasons on a sheet of newsprint, and tape it to the wall. Ask:

● **What does this list tell you about war?** *(Wars happen for many different reasons; people fight for stupid reasons.)*

Say: **Wars happen for many different reasons and are rarely simple matters. Even in the Bible, we can see a variety of reasons nations went to war. Let's look at a couple of examples in the Old Testament.**

Form two teams. Give each team three marshmallows per person, and have the teams stand on opposite sides of the room.

Say: **I'm going read a couple of Scripture passages and then ask a question for each one. The first person to raise his or her hand gets to answer the question. If that person is correct, his or her team gets to pelt the other team with marshmallows. If that person is wrong, his or her team gets pelted by the other team.**

Read aloud Joshua 10:1-5. Then ask:

● **Why did the Amorites go to war with Gibeon?**

The correct answer is because the Amorites feared Gibeon's might. If the guesser is correct, have his or her teammates each toss one marshmallow at the other team. If the guesser is incorrect, have the members of the other team each toss one marshmallow at the guesser's team.

Then read aloud 2 Samuel 10:1-7. Ask:

● **Why did the Ammonites go to war with David?** (Answer: The Ammonites distrusted David's intentions.)

Read aloud James 4:1-6. Say: **Beginning with the first team to have all its teammates sit down, we'll alternate having teams explain reasons people go to war based on this or the other two passages we read. You'll have ten seconds to call out a reason. If you can't think of a reason, the other team will get to toss the rest of its marshmallows at you.**

Students might list reasons such as pride, distrust, fear, greed, or lust. When one team can't think of a reason within ten seconds, have the other team toss its marshmallows.

Have students pick up the marshmallows and throw them away. Then form a circle. Ask:

● **What were your feelings when you were pelted with marshmallows?** *(I felt silly; it was humiliating; it didn't bother me; it made me upset.)*

● **How are these feelings like the way people might feel if they're in a war?** *(People in the middle of a war would be angry; people in a war would be more upset.)*

Say: **The book of James has a keen insight into the reasons people go to war. Quarrels or fights occur out of pride or greed. And while two or more nations fight for pride or property, still other nations may try to step in and help solve the conflict. The more nations that get involved in a war, the more complex it becomes. And while it's true that the Old Testament is packed with wars that seem to be ordained by God, God doesn't want us to be a warring people. Instead, God calls us to be patient, giving, and peaceful in dealing with others.**

PIECES OF THE PIE

Cut apart these slips, and give one to each group.

| **Why You Need the Pie** You need seven starred pie pieces because they could help your country get out of an economic depression. | **Why You Need the Pie** You need seven pie pieces with triangles because you need them to be in control of the nations that surround you. | **Why You Need the Pie** You need seven pie pieces with circles because your country's religious beliefs say these pie pieces belong to your people. |

PIE CHART

PIE RULES

The object of this game is to collect seven pie pieces with the symbol described on your "Why You Need the Pie" slip. You may use any of the following strategies to get pie pieces:

● You may negotiate with other groups to give you pie pieces.

● You may trade with other groups for pie pieces you want.

● You may trick other groups into giving you pie pieces.

● You may steal other groups' pie pieces. But remember: Torn pie pieces aren't worth anything.

● You may declare war against another group. Read the following rules for war.

If you declare war, here are the steps you must take:

1. You must state your reasons for declaring war.

2. Each group must roll a die to see who wins the battles in the war. The group that rolls the higher number wins one pie piece from the other group. If both groups' rolls are the same, they each lose a pie piece to the group not in the battle. The war ends only when both groups agree to end it or when one group is completely out of pie pieces.

No Winners

Purpose:
Students will explore God's expectations of families.

Supplies:
You'll need Bibles, sets of dominoes, newsprint, markers, and tape.

Experience:

Form "family" groups of no more than four, each consisting of one or two "parents" and up to three "children." Ask each family to send you one representative. Take the representatives aside or outside of the room and say: **I'm going to give each of you a set of dominoes. Take them to your family and explain that you're supposed to work together to build a tower. The family that builds the highest tower in three minutes wins. I'll cough just before the three minutes are up. That's your secret signal to say something like, "I don't like this dumb tower," and knock the tower over. Don't let on that this is a planned demolition.**

Have the representatives return to their families with the dominoes. Give the signal for the beginning of the three-minute building period. Emphasize that there's enough time to do a careful job. Just before the three minutes are up, give the coughing signal.

As students begin to accuse you of setting up the activity for failure, say: **You all know what happened here. I set up this activity to self-destruct.** Ask:

● **What were your reactions when your representative suddenly destroyed your tower?** *(I thought, "Oh, great!"; I figured something like this would happen.)*

● **How is this self-destruction like what sometimes happens in families?** *(It only takes one person's negative attitude to ruin things for everyone else.)*

Say: **One of the most remarkable things about families is that we often save our worst behavior for those we love the most. Here's some simple proof. Turn to the people in your family group and tell them two compliments you've given recently to people in your real-life family.**

Allow a few moments for sharing. Then say: **Now tell the people in your group about two negative comments you've made recently to people in your real-life family.**

After a few more moments, call everyone together, and ask:

● **Which was easier to think of—compliments you'd given or nega-tive comments?**

● **Why do you think we often save our worst behavior for those who are closest to us?** *(We know they'll love us no matter how we behave; dumping is a two-way street—they do it to us, so we do it to them.)*

● **How do you think the atmosphere in your family would change if everyone made an attempt to be positive and affirming?** *(That's an im-possible dream; if everyone really worked at it, it might make a big difference.)*

Say: **We don't want to turn our families into places where nobody wins. One person's positive effort can make a big difference in how a family feels. And we know that our families are worth that kind of ef-fort because the Bible places high value on families. Let's take a few minutes to discover how and why families got started and what God expects from families today.**

Tape a large sheet of newsprint onto the wall. With a marker, write at the top of the newsprint, "Who needs families?" Then say: **Let's make a list of things our families supply for us. We'll go around the room, and each family can add one thing at a time to the list.**

Have families take turns adding to the list until everyone is out of ideas. Then say: **We've made a pretty significant list of things we depend on our families to provide for us. Now let's choose the top five items on the list. Of all these things listed here, which would you least want to do without?**

Put a star by each of the items students suggest. Then say: **Let's go to the Bible to discover God's priorities for families.**

Have a volunteer read aloud Genesis 2:18-24. Then ask:

● **From God's perspective, what important human needs does a family meet?** *(The need for companionship, help, and a sense of belonging.)*

Jot down students' responses in a second list.

Have another volunteer read Deuteronomy 6:1-9 aloud. Again ask:

● **From God's perspective, what important human needs does a family meet?** *(The need for learning about God's love and God's rules; the need to learn discipline and obedience; the need to live in a peaceful, prosperous com-munity.)*

After you've listed students' responses, say: Let's compare our two lists. Ask:

● **How closely does our list of needs compare to the needs we found in the two Bible passages?** *(They're pretty close; we were way off.)*

Say: **Families are usually far from perfect. But we can improve our families if we simply take a look at God's perspective on families and begin to apply what we discover.**

Playing to Lose

Purpose:
Students will learn that when they hurt people, they need to ask forgiveness for their actions.

Supplies:
You'll need a Bible, index cards, markers, candy, newsprint, and tape.

Experience:
Prepare forty index cards for this activity. Number cards from one to ten, with one number on each card. Use a different-colored marker for each complete set of ten cards. When you finish, you'll have cards numbered from one to ten in four different colors.

Form four teams. Ask each team to select a team Captain. Tell students they'll be playing a game with the cards you've made.

Say: **Each team will try to be the first to get the cards from one to ten of the same color.**

The team Captain must keep the team's hand of cards. Other team members will each take one card at a time from their Captain to other teams to trade for another card. Team members can then bring the cards back to their Captain, and he or she will give them each another card to trade.

The Captain may also trade cards.

Each member of the winning team will receive a piece of candy. At the end of five minutes, if no team has gotten ten cards of one color, the team with the most cards of one color will win.

Before the game begins, take the team Captains out of the room. Tell them: **Your job is to work against your team. You must try to keep your team from getting many cards of the same color. Trade away cards if you see that you're getting close to winning.** Tell Captains not to tell their teams they'll be working against them.

Shuffle the cards, and distribute the cards among the teams. Students may move all over the room trying to trade cards for whatever colors their teams decide to collect.

At the end of five minutes, call time. Ask Captains to find the card colors they have the most of and count those cards. Give a piece of candy to each student on the team with the most cards of one color.

Explain to the group: **You may not have known it, but your Captains were working against you throughout this game. While you were working on getting cards of the same color, your Captains were trading those cards away.** Ask:

● **What are your initial thoughts about the way your Captains worked against you?** *(I don't like it; it doesn't bother me; I'm upset, I wanted the candy.)*

● **How well does a team work when one player is working against the team?** *(Not very well, the whole team must work together to succeed; it depends—if the team is strong, one weak link won't hurt it much.)*

Ask the Captains:

● **What was it like to work against your teammates?** *(I felt uncomfortable; I felt like a spy.)*

● **How did you feel when your team lost because of your efforts?** *(Upset; sad; distressed.)*

● **How is that like the way people feel when they disappoint or hurt someone else?** *(They feel bad; they probably feel upset about what they've done.)*

Say: **In this activity, I "hurt" the Captains' reputations by making them cheat their own teams. And the Captains hurt their teams' chances of winning by trading away important cards. When we hurt people, we need to ask forgiveness for our actions.**

Ask the Captains to forgive you for making them cheat their teammates. Have Captains ask their teammates to forgive them for trying to make them lose. Ask:

● **Is it easy to ask forgiveness for something you've done that hurt someone? Why or why not?** *(No, it's humbling to ask for forgiveness; no, you don't know how people will respond; yes, if you really feel bad, it's easy to ask for forgiveness.)*

Say: **It can be painful and humiliating to ask forgiveness for our errors. But we all do things that require us to ask for forgiveness. Even the greatest Bible characters had to deal with similar feelings.**

Assume that we're all guards and servants in the palace of King David. All of us believe that David is a good king and a man who followed God. For now, try to forget everything you may have heard about the sins David committed. We are all in the hall of the palace. The prophet Nathan has asked to see the king, and the prophet has been admitted. Everyone waits to hear what he will say.

Ask students to listen as a volunteer reads aloud 2 Samuel 12:1-13.

Have another volunteer retell the story as if he or she had heard Nathan firsthand and is telling friends about what just happened. Then ask:

● **What are your reactions to these words from the prophet Nathan?** *(I'm surprised; I'm angry; it makes me upset; I'm confused.)*

● **Who was hurt by David?** *(Bathsheba; Uriah; anyone who respected David.)*

● **What led David to hurt these people so badly?** *(Lust; his desire for Bathsheba; greed.)*

● **Think of times in your life when you've done things to hurt others. How did you feel?** *(Disappointed; sad; upset.)*

Tape a sheet of newsprint to the wall. Distribute markers. Ask one student to read Psalm 51:1-12 aloud. Explain that this passage was likely David's prayer after Nathan had confronted him.

Say: **In this prayer, David asked God to forgive him for his sin.** Ask:

● **Who else did David need to seek forgiveness from?** *(Uriah; Bathsheba; Nathan.)*

● **What thoughts from David's prayer might be important in asking the forgiveness of another person?** *(Admit the wrong; express regret; ask for forgiveness.)*

Have a volunteer list students' ideas on the newsprint.

Say: **David knew that even though he'd really hurt Bathsheba and Uriah, his sin was really against God.** Ask:

● **Why do our actions against other people affect our relationship with God?** *(When we hurt others, we're also hurting God.)*

Have a volunteer read aloud James 5:16. Ask:

● **What does this verse mean?** *(We should support one another when we mess up; we need to confess our sins to other people.)*

Say: **When we mess up or hurt other people, we need to ask forgiveness from the people we hurt—and from God.**

Putting It All Together

Purpose

Students will discover that God wants to have an intimate relationship with each of them.

Supplies:

You'll need a Bible, six copies of the "Twenty-Four-Piece Puzzle" handout (p. 80), scissors, newsprint, markers, and tape.

Experience:

Form seven groups. (A group can be one person.) Give six of the groups each a cut-apart photocopy of the "Twenty-Four-Piece Puzzle" handout (p. 80). Give the seventh group a different piece from each of the puzzles (so there is only one piece missing from each of the other groups' puzzles). Tell the seventh group to watch the others struggle to put together the puzzles, which can only be completed with the help of the seventh group. Allow the groups with puzzles to reach a point of frustration.

After several minutes, allow students in the seventh group to go around and help the other groups complete their puzzles. Ask the groups with puzzles:

● **What went through your mind when you couldn't do your puzzle on your own?** (I was frustrated; I thought we'd been cheated.)

Ask the seventh group:

● **What were you thinking while you were watching the other groups try to finish their puzzles on their own?** (Like I was in on a secret; like I was in control; I wanted them to hurry so I could fix it for them.)

Ask the groups with puzzles:

● **Once you found out where to go for the missing piece, how did you feel about asking someone else for help?** (It was no big deal; it was frustrating.)

Ask the seventh group:

● **How did you feel when the other groups were asking you for help?** (Like I had a lot of power; like I was needed.)

● **How would you react if you knew the others wouldn't come to you for help even though they needed you?** *(I'd feel frustrated; I wouldn't like it.)*

Say: **All through history, God has been trying to tell us that he wants to have a relationship with each of us. Not just as a ruler or a judge, but as an intimate friend.**

Read aloud Proverbs 18:24. Ask:

● **How can a friend be closer than a brother?** *(Some friends listen to you better than even family members do; some friends stick with you in tough times, even when your family doesn't.)*

● **How is God like the friend in Proverbs 18:24?** *(God always listens; God loves you as you are; God is always there for you.)*

● **How could you be a friend to God like the friend in Proverbs 18:24?** *(I could work harder at listening to and obeying God; I could stick by what I know God wants, no matter what.)*

Read aloud John 15:13-15. Ask:

● **What sort of things do you think people who want to be Jesus' friends will do, according to this passage?** *(They'll do what Jesus wants them to do; they'll take care of each other.)*

● **How does Jesus show us he is our friend?** *(He died for us; he wants us to be his friends, not just his servants.)*

Tape a large sheet of newsprint to the wall. Make plenty of markers available to your group. Have students create a mural to illustrate how Jesus is the ultimate friend. Encourage them to think both in terms of what Jesus did in New Testament times to prove his friendship and how his friendship affects their lives today. Try to allow enough time to let them feel as though they've produced a quality piece of work.

Say: **You did a wonderful job of illustrating Jesus' friendship. One big thing we can learn from Jesus' example is sacrifice. Friends make sacrifices for each other. Jesus is the ultimate example of that, and that's why we can believe him when he says he's our friend.**

Twenty-Four-Piece Puzzle

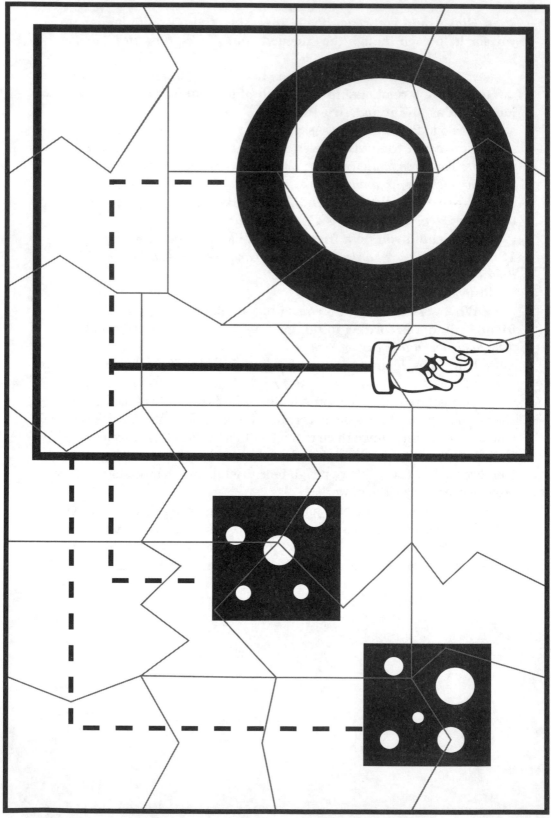

Rat Race

Purpose:

Students will discover that both giving support and receiving support are necessary to build a healthy family.

Supplies:

You'll need Bibles, index cards, markers, masking tape, hymnals, individually wrapped chocolate candies, and newsprint.

Experience:

Before class, write stress-related illnesses such as gastric ulcers, migraine headaches, nervous breakdowns, and heart disease on index cards. You'll need one illness card for every four students. Mark a starting line with masking tape about three feet from one end of the room. Form teams of four, and have each team choose one member to be the Parent. Give each team a hymnal and three chocolate candies. Line the teams up single file behind the starting line. Place a chair at the other end of the room opposite each team.

Say: **This is a rat race, and here's how it works. Each team will balance its hymnal on the head of its Parent. The Parent will hold the chocolate candies as he or she walks to the other end of the room, circles the chair, and comes back to his or her team. Still balancing the book, the Parent will unwrap the chocolate candies, place one candy in the mouth of each team member, walk to the other end of the room again, circle the chair again, and then return to the team. OK, Parents, heads up! Teams, balance your books.**

When a book is balanced on each Parent's head, say: **Go!** Encourage the teams to cheer their Parents on. Each time a Parent drops a book, have him or her stop and replace the book before starting again.

At the end of the race, give all the Parents a round of applause. Ask the students who sat on the sidelines:

● **What went through your mind as your Parent struggled to finish the race?** *(I felt sorry for our team's Parent; I wished I could've helped.)*

Ask the Parents:

● **What was it like to balance the book, run the race, and feed your children?** *(It was tricky; I didn't think I could pull it off.)*

Now ask the whole group:

● **How is this like what happens in real families?** *(Parents have to balance a lot of responsibilities, and we can't always do a lot to help.)*

Say: **Oh—I almost forgot. I have rewards for all the Parents.** Pass out one illness card you prepared before class to each Parent. Ask:

● **Are these the kinds of rewards real parents earn? Explain.** *(Yes, if they don't get help and support from their kids; no, my parents know how to take care of themselves.)*

Say: **Let's name practical ways you can support your parents to keep them from earning the kinds of rewards I just passed out. Each suggestion you give earns you a chocolate candy.** Record students' responses on the left side of a sheet of newsprint. Ask:

● **Turning the tables, what can your parents do to support you?**
Record these responses on the right side of the same sheet of newsprint. Ask:

● **What's similar about these lists? What's different?**

● **What happens if family members on one side feel like they're doing all of the giving and none of the receiving?** *(Tension and resentment builds.)*

● **How does God want you to support your family?**

● **How does God want your family to support you?**
Read aloud Ephesians 6:1-4.

Say: **The giving and receiving of support needs to be a two-way street. That's what keeps family members working together.**

Repeat After Me

Purpose:
Students will examine how listening leads to greater understanding.

Supplies:
You'll need Bibles, a potato, newsprint, and markers.

Experience:

Form a circle. Tell students you're going to have a hot potato discussion about communicating with parents. Ask students each to think about the thing that's hardest about communicating with parents and the thing that's easiest about it.

Before you begin the discussion, hold up the potato and explain that it will be tossed to students in random order as they share their responses. Also explain that before each student speaks, he or she must restate what the previous student said. This will encourage students to really listen to others' responses. Toss the potato to someone to start the discussion.

After everyone has shared, ask:

● **What was it like to have to listen carefully to what other group members were saying?** *(It was easy, I usually do anyway; it was difficult, I was listening so hard I forgot what I was going to say.)*

● **How did it feel to have others listening carefully to your words? Explain.** *(Awkward, I was in the spotlight; important, they wanted to hear what I said.)*

● **How would school, home, or other activities be different if people always listened this way?** *(We would understand each other better; we wouldn't argue so much.)*

● **What has this experience taught you about being a better listener?** *(Listening is fun; I don't need to worry about what I'm going to say all the time; it's good to repeat what someone else says so I get it right.)*

Say: **Listening leads to greater understanding. It helps avoid fights and lets others know you really care about them.**

Form two groups—the "Jesus" group and the "Pilate" group. Give each group a Bible, newsprint, and a marker. Have a student in the Jesus group write "Jesus' Perspective" at the top of the group's newsprint, and have a student in the Pilate group write "Pilate's Perspective" at the top of the group's newsprint.

Say: **In this passage, Pilate never really understood what Jesus was telling him. I'll assign each group a different perspective to read this passage from.**

Say to the Jesus group: **Read John 18:33-38. Then write the message you think Jesus was trying to convey to Pilate.**

Say to the Pilate group: **Read John 18:33-38. Then write what you think Pilate was hearing Jesus say.**

When groups are ready, have them each tell what they wrote. Ask:

● **What kept Pilate from really hearing what Jesus was telling him?** *(He saw Jesus as a threat to his power; he didn't really understand or ask more about Jesus' perspective.)*

● **What sometimes keeps us from really hearing others?** *(We've already made up our minds about what they're talking about; we don't really care what they're saying; we're distracted by other things around us.)*

Have a volunteer read aloud Mark 4:24-25. Ask:

● **What does this passage tell us about the value of listening?** *(The way I listen to others is probably the way others listen to me; a person who listens will gain more understanding; a person who doesn't listen will lose the understanding he or she already has.)*

● **How easy or difficult is it to listen to God? Explain.** *(It's easy to listen, but I don't always know what God is saying; it's tough because I don't usually like what I hear.)*

● **What are some things a good listener does?** *(Gives you his or her full attention; asks questions.)*

● **Based on what we've talked about so far, do you think you are a good listener? Why or why not?** *(Yes, I really enjoy getting involved with other people; no, I have a hard time concentrating on what is said.)*

● **What are some other things we can do to become better listeners?** *(Don't talk as much; make eye contact.)*

Say: **With a little effort and by using the tips we've discussed today, all of us can learn to be better listeners. Not only will those around us benefit, but we'll be better off, too.**

Respect

Purpose:

Students will explore what the Bible says about favoritism.

Supplies:

You'll need Bibles, one copy of the "Respect Bowl" handout (p. 88) and one copy of the "Game Cards and Parts" handout (p. 89) for each group of ten, scissors, a bowl, one doughnut for each student, and napkins.

Experience:

Note: Before you lead this lesson, you'll need to evaluate whether you play favorites with the people in your group. Be honest with yourself. Do you spend time outside of youth group talking with particular friends more than others? This lesson may bring out feelings in others who have felt slighted by you. Be prepared to apologize if you need to.

If your group is larger than ten, create groups of no more than ten and follow the instructions below for each group. You'll need a volunteer to be the Rulemaster (one for each group). For groups smaller than ten, do the activity as one group.

Cut apart the Respect Cards, the Disrespect Cards, and the Number Slips from the "Game Cards and Parts" handout (p. 89). Place the Respect Cards and the Disrespect Cards face down in separate piles. Fold the Number Slips each in half, and place them in a bowl.

Have each group sit in a circle on the floor. Place the Respect Bowl game board, the Respect Cards, the Disrespect Cards, and the Number-Slips bowl in the center of the circle. Place one doughnut on a napkin in front of each student. Tell students not to eat the doughnuts; they're part of the game. Have students each find a playing piece—for example, they may use a coin, an earring, a key, a paper wad, or a paper clip.

Say: **We're going to play the Respect Bowl game. Each person will, in turn, draw one Number Slip from the bowl and move his or her playing piece the appropriate number of spaces on the board. If someone lands on a Respect space or a Disrespect space, he or she must take a card from the appropriate pile and do what it says. The game is over when someone goes around the board once and reaches Start. The only other rule is that the Rulemaster may change the rules at any** time. **If you don't like a rule the Rulemaster has changed, you may protest—but the Rulemaster may or may not change his or her mind.**

Have the Rulemaster secretly choose two or three game-players to give special favors to. Have the Rulemaster change the rules for those people to make sure they always get the best possible moves. For example, if a favorite person lands on a Disrespect space, the Rulemaster may tell that player to draw a Respect Card instead. Or if a favored player picks a "one" Number Slip, the Rulemaster may tell the player to move five spaces instead. Other players will probably complain. Have the Rulemaster give in to their complaints and reverse a decision at least once during the game. But be sure the favorite players continue to get preferential treatment.

Have the person who's wearing the most colorful shoes go first. As the Respect Cards and Disrespect Cards are drawn, have players replace them at the bottom of each pile. During the game, if students are asked to move the doughnuts around, make sure they use their napkins so they don't end up touching all the doughnuts. After someone wins the game, tell students they can eat the doughnuts. Ask:

● **What went through your mind when the Rulemaster made it easier for some players to win?** *(It was unfair; I felt angry; I was upset.)*

● **How did you feel when the Rulemaster listened to your complaints and reversed a decision? Explain.** *(Great, I was glad the Rulemaster listened; good, it made me feel like my input was important.)*

● **How open was the Rulemaster to your complaints about showing favoritism?** *(Not very open; somewhat open.)*

● **How is this like the way parents, friends, or teachers might respond to your concerns about their favoritism?** *(My friends are open to listening to me; teachers won't listen to my concerns; my parents might listen, but they won't always agree with me.)*

● **Do people always know they're playing favorites? Why or why not?** *(Yes, they usually do it to make others feel bad; no, they don't usually think about it.)*

● **How do you feel when people play favorites?** *(Angry; upset; it doesn't bother me.)*

● **Why do people show favoritism?** *(Because they like the way certain people look or think; because they don't know any better.)*

● **How is showing favoritism different from having a "best friend"?** *(Favoritism excludes other people; it's not much different.)*

Say: **Favoritism creates negative feelings and hurts relationships. Yet you have probably seen friends, teachers, or parents show favoritism. And whether you were the "favorite" or the "outsider" in those situations, you probably felt uncomfortable about the preferential treatment.**

Form two groups. Assign one of the following passages to each group: Genesis 25:24-28; 27:1-35 or Genesis 37:3-5, 18-28. Have groups each read their passage and create a skit based on the passage. Tell groups their skits should be modern-day versions of the stories. For example, the Genesis 37 skit could be about a brother who is given more freedom than his siblings and is picked on by his brothers and sisters.

Have each group present its skit. After each skit, have students briefly discuss how they felt as participants in the skit. Then discuss how these biblical situations are similar to favoritism students experience today. Ask:

● **How would you have felt as Joseph? Joseph's brothers? Jacob? Esau?**

● **What can we do to help friends, family members, or teachers keep from playing favorites?** *(Confront them about the issue; tell them how you feel.)*

Have someone read aloud Proverbs 8:17. Ask:

● **Does God have favorite people? Why or why not?** *(Yes, Christians are his favorites; no, he loves everyone the same.)*

● **How does it feel to be loved by God?** *(Great; fantastic; good.)*

Say: **God's boundless love makes each one of us his favorite. But we live in a world where some people don't treat others fairly. We can confront favoritism when we see it, but we can't always change the way people think or act toward others. When we feel less than favored by friends, family, or others, we can always know we're still God's favorites.**

Respect Bowl

START ⬇

Take a Respect Card

Take a Disrespect Card

Take a Respect Card

Take a Disrespect Card

Take a Respect Card

Take a Disrespect Card

Take a Respect Card

Take a Disrespect Card

Take a Respect Card

Take a Disrespect Card

Take a Respect Card

Take a Disrespect Card

Take a Respect Card

Take a Disrespect Card

Game Cards and Parts

Number Slips

| 1 | 2 | 3 | 4 |

Disrespect Cards

Disrespect Card

Lose one turn.

Disrespect Card

Go back three spaces.

Disrespect Card

Give all your doughnuts to the person on your left.

Disrespect Card

Go back to Start.

Disrespect Card

Lose one turn.

Disrespect Card

Go back three spaces.

Disrespect Card

Give all your doughnuts to the person on your left.

Disrespect Card

Go back five spaces.

Respect Cards

Respect Card

Take one doughnut from any other player.

Respect Card

Move ahead three spaces.

Respect Card

Take one extra turn.

Respect Card

Move ahead two spaces.

Respect Card

Take one doughnut from any other player.

Respect Card

Move ahead three spaces.

Respect Card

Take one extra turn.

Respect Card

Move ahead five spaces.

Shoe Churches

Purpose:

Students will learn that each Christian denomination illustrates the truth of the gospel differently.

Supplies:

You'll need Bibles, newsprint, markers, and chairs or sheets and thumbtacks.

Experience:

Have students each remove their shoes and place them into one of the following piles: white tennis shoes, other-colored tennis shoes, sandals, loafers, and other types of shoes. Place the piles in various locations in the room.

Have students each stand next to the pile of shoes they think is the best type of shoe. Then have groups each defend their choice by explaining why that type of shoe is best and why the others are inferior. Encourage groups to huddle together and become more adamant about their choices as they defend their favorite shoe styles.

As students debate the advantages and disadvantages of each shoe type, begin to separate the groups by putting chairs between them or, if possible, hanging sheets from the ceiling between them. After a few minutes, each group should be totally separated from the other groups. Ask:

● **What is it like to be separated from the other groups?** *(It's kind of strange; I thought it was appropriate since we were arguing; it feels right.)*

● **How is the way groups were separated over their favorite shoe styles like the way groups are separated because of different theologies or church traditions? How is it different?** *(It's similar because people are always fighting about differences; it's different because people don't really argue like this.)*

● **What did you think about having to choose only one type of shoe?** *(It was hard; I thought it was unrealistic.)*

● **What would life be like if we could own only one pair of shoes?** *(Dull; uncomfortable.)*

● **How are the different groups of shoes like different Christian churches?** *(They all have one purpose; they are all different in some ways and alike in others.)*

● **How would you feel if everybody had to believe exactly the same things in order to go to church?** *(Angry; worried.)*

● **How is the need for different types of shoes like the need for different kinds of Christian churches?** *(Different churches work best in different environments; it takes different kinds of churches to reach different kinds of people.)*

Say: **Although the shoes individually belong to different groups, we need all of them to complete the "family" of shoes. Likewise, Christians belong to many different churches but they are all needed to complete the family of God.**

Form groups of no more than four. Give groups each a sheet of newsprint, markers, and a Bible. Have groups each read Ephesians 4:1-7 and then draw a poster that illustrates the passage in some way.

When groups are finished, have them explain their illustrations. Then ask:

● **What made you decide to illustrate the passage in this way?** *(This is the way we pictured these verses; this reflects what we think these verses mean.)*

Say: **Look around at the other illustrations. They aren't like yours, even though they illustrate the same passage.** Then ask:

● **Are the other illustrations wrong? Why or why not?** *(No, they just focus on a different part of the passage; no, they just express the same thing in a different way.)*

● **How is that like different denominations in the Christian faith?** *(They're all different expressions of the same thing; they each emphasize different aspects of the same truth.)*

Say: **Just as each of your pictures illustrates the same passage differently, so each Christian denomination illustrates the truth of the gospel differently. We can see from this experience that it is possible for denominations to be different and yet all be right.**

Trust or Consequences

Purpose:

Students will explore the importance of building their parents' trust in them.

Supplies:

You'll need Bibles, a water balloon, a box of straight pins, one copy of the "Trust Check" handout (p. 94) for each person, and pencils.

Experience:

Sit in a chair in the middle of the room, and place a water balloon on your lap. Tell students there's a small box of straight pins on a table on the other side of the room.

Say: **Raise your hand if I can trust you to walk around me three times with a pin in your hand and not prick this balloon.** Get students' responses about whether they think they could do it.

Say: **If you know you can't be trusted, raise your hand.**

Have the self-proclaimed trustworthy students get straight pins and form a line, ready to march around you in a circle.

Say: **OK, I'm going to close my eyes, and I want you to walk around me three times slowly with your pins in hand. Then sit down again.**

Be prepared for whatever transpires—bring an extra skirt or pair of pants and a towel for cleanup. Your lap may be wet or dry when students sit back down. There is some risk here! In either case, use these questions to debrief. Ask:

● **How did it feel to be trusted with something that could possibly bring pain or disappointment to another person?** *(It feels good to be trusted; I liked the feeling of power and tension.)*

● **How did it feel to have and keep someone's trust** (or to lose someone's trust)**?**

Responses will depend on whether someone pricked the water balloon. If someone did, make sure students know this was a fun activity, that you brought a change of clothes, and that no one needs to feel guilty. Probably the balloon-buster will let you know just how much fun it was! Ask:

● **How is this activity like conflicts between you and your parents?** *(My parents act like it's a big risk to trust me with small things; it seems like my parents expect me to fail—just like you expected us to fail and brought a change of clothes.)*

Say: **Was there anybody here who didn't want this balloon to get popped? Who would want to miss all that fun, excitement, and humiliation? Many times, parents withhold their trust because they worry that in a tempting situation, their kids are going to go for the excitement. The Bible's approach to this issue of obedience and trust is interesting because it speaks to both parents and kids.**

Give students each a photocopy of the "Trust Check" handout (p. 94), a pencil, and a Bible. Have students work through the top half of the handout individually. Then have students pair up to role play the steps for establishing trust in a conflict area.

Say: **You and your partner will take turns being parents to each other. Begin by reading Ephesians 6:1-4 aloud together. Then tell your partner the conflict area you identified on your handout. Take turns playing the role of a parent and talk with your "child" about that area. Try to identify with your partners' needs and feelings.**

Afterward, ask:

● **What was it like to play the role of a parent? What new insights did you discover?** *(Parents aren't really trying to be mean, they have needs and wants too; it's probably easier to give in to kids than to make rules stick.)*

● **What do you think would happen if you tried the ideas you practiced in this role-play in real life?** *(It might work; my parents would never trust me.)*

Have students each say something positive to the whole group about their partner's insights in this activity. For example, someone might say, "You really had a good idea about how parents see things" or "I like the ideas you came up with."

Say: **Parents aren't always in the right. Sometimes they mess up and do things for the wrong reasons. According to 1 Corinthians 13:5, love "keeps no record of wrongs." By trying to see things the way your parents see them, you can discover new ways to build trust.**

TRUST

Put a star in each box below if you have your parents' trust in this area. Put an X in the box if this is a conflict area between you and your parents. Be prepared to role play with a partner one of the conflict areas.

- ☐ How I handle my money
- ☐ My choice of friends
- ☐ Getting home when I say I will
- ☐ Caring for younger brothers or sisters
- ☐ Being with people of the opposite sex

- ☐ Dressing appropriately
- ☐ Getting my homework done
- ☐ Being home alone
- ☐ Going shopping on my own
- ☐ Watching television responsibly

CHECK

I'd really like to improve my parents' trust in me in this area:

X

Read Ephesians 6:1-4. Then role play the steps below with a "parent" partner to improve the trust level in the area you just identified. Begin a conversation with your partner similar to the one listed. Then have your partner respond as a parent might actually respond.

Step One: Give Trust

1. Clearly state your point of view, your needs, and your wants. Tell how your feelings relate to your requests. For example, you might say, "I'm upset you don't let me stay out later…"
2. Listen carefully to understand the needs and wants of your parent. Find out how your parent's feelings relate to the decisions about rules and restrictions.

Step Two: Ask for Trust

1. Find out what you could do to gain your parent's trust. Ask your parent to suggest possibilities. Discuss them. Agree to start doing one of the things suggested. For example, you might ask, "What can I do to build trust with you?" or "What can I do to help you see that I'm responsible?"
2. Set a definite date and time for a follow-up conference. Talk about your performance so far.

X

Twisted Trivia

Purpose:

Students will explore the issue of prejudice.

Supplies:

You'll need a Bible, two pieces of poster board, markers, paper, and pencils.

Experience:

Prepare two signs on the pieces of poster board, one with the word "Applause" written on it and the other with the word "Boo" written on it.

Form two teams based on students' birthdays. Team A should have those people born from January through June. Team B should have those born from July through December. It's OK to have uneven numbers.

Tell students they're going to play Bible trivia. Do not tell them, however, that you are prejudiced against Team A and will be reading that team extremely hard questions while giving easy questions to Team B. Further discriminate against Team A by giving members little time to answer, by dropping hints to Team B, and by praising Team B exclusively. Be sure you don't single out or embarrass any one player from either team, especially Team A.

Use the trivia questions from the box below to play the game. The answers are located in parentheses after the questions.

Trivia Questions

TEAM A

1. Who is the "Queen of Heaven"? (A pagan goddess referenced in Jeremiah 7:18.)
2. Under which empire did Ezekiel prophesy? (Babylonian, Ezekiel 1:3.)
3. Where did Moses' sister Miriam die? (Kadesh, Numbers 20:1.)
4. When Israel's enemies outnumbered them, which plant did Asaph say God would make the enemies like? (Tumbleweed, Psalm 83:13.)
5. What is Mount Hermon called by the Sidonians? (Sirion, Deuteronomy 3:9.)

TEAM B

1. What is the first book in the Bible? (Genesis.)
2. What did Noah build before the floods came? (The ark.)
3. Who was Adam's mate? (Eve.)
4. Who was the mother of Jesus? (Mary.)
5. On which object was Jesus crucified? (A cross.)

After the game, ask:

● **What was it like to be a member of Team A?** *(Unfair; frustrating.)*

● **What was it like to be a member of Team B?** *(Fun; unchallenging.)*

● **What were your thoughts when you figured out the game wasn't fair?** *(I wanted to quit; I decided to complain.)*

● **How was this game like real life?** *(Sometimes people do unfair things to other people; some people have it easier than others.)*

Say: **There are people all over the world who are treated unfairly just because their skin is a different color, they speak a different language, or they come from a different land. Treating people badly for reasons such as these is just as wrong as favoring one team over another in the trivia game we played. Let's look at what Jesus has to say about racism and prejudice.**

One group of New Testament people that was often treated unfairly was the Samaritans. The Jews hated them because Samaritan people were descended from a mixture of Jews and Gentiles (non-Jews). As a result, they were looked down upon and ridiculed for not being as "good" as the Jewish people. However, Jesus saw them in a different light. Let's take a look at a story he told about a Samaritan.

Ask for volunteers to act out the story of the good Samaritan in Luke 10:30-37. You'll need a traveler, a couple of robbers, a priest, a Levite, a Samaritan, a donkey, and an innkeeper. Also select two students who will hold up the signs saying "Applause" and "Boo" as cue cards for the remaining group members (or students who currently aren't acting in the role-play). It's OK for students to play more than one role if your group is smaller than ten.

Read aloud "The Good Samaritan" story from the box on page 97, having students act out their parts and giving directions to the sign-holders as you go.

The Good Samaritan

(based on Luke 10:30-37)

A traveler was going down from Jerusalem to Jericho (applause) when he fell into the hands of robbers (boo). They stripped him of his clothes, beat him, and went away, leaving him half-dead (boo). A priest, well-respected and very religious, happened to be going down the same road (applause). When he saw the man, he passed by on the other side (boo).

So too, a Levite, who came from a good and influential family, was going down the road (applause). When he came to the place and saw the man, he passed by on the other side (boo).

A Samaritan, one who was disliked by the Jews, also came by. He had been treated poorly by Jewish people in the past because he was from Samaria.

However, as he traveled, the Samaritan came to where the man was; when he saw him, he took pity on him (applause). He went to him and bandaged his wounds (applause). Then he put the man on his own donkey, took him to an inn, and took care of him (applause). The next day, the Samaritan took out two silver coins and gave them to the innkeeper. "Look after him," he said, "and when I return, I will reimburse you for any extra expense you may have" (applause).

After the story, ask:

● **What might have gone through your mind if you were the man on the side of the road?** *(I'd have felt discouraged; I'd have wondered why no one would help me.)*

● **Why do you think the priest and the Levite passed by?** *(They didn't have time; they didn't want to deal with the situation.)*

● **Why do you think the Samaritan stopped to help someone who was probably a Jew and supposedly hated Samaritans?** *(He didn't care which nationality he was; he saw a need and felt compassion.)*

● **How are the people in this story like people we know today?** *(Everyone is prejudiced against someone; people don't seem to care about others anymore.)*

Say: **People still hate others because of race, just as they did back in New Testament days. But prejudice goes beyond racism alone. We can be prejudiced against the rich, the talented, or the ugly and "nerdy" people. Let's discover some other groups that may experience prejudice today.**

Brainstorm with students about the different types of "crowds" at their schools, such as nerds, athletes, socialites, rich students, and students with disabilities. Then read Colossians 3:11 aloud. After you read the verse, give students each a sheet of paper and a pencil. Have students each act as a "ghostwriter" and rewrite the passage the way Paul might have written it if he'd had these new crowds in mind. Have volunteers read their rewritten verses to the whole group.

Then ask:

● **How would Paul respond to the prejudice you see in your school?** *(He would speak out against it; he would be angry.)*

● **What do you know about God that would support how you think he feels about racism and prejudice?** *(God hates injustice; God is fair.)*

● **How can you respond to the prejudice you see in your school?** *(I can speak out against it; I can try to include everybody in my circle of friends.)*

Say: **Prejudice is hard to ignore when it affects you directly. But it can be easy to overlook when it's aimed at someone else. Yet prejudice will only come to an end when you and I do what we can to stay free from prejudice and to help others get free from it too.**

Universal Prejudice

Purpose:

Students will explore ways to avoid stereotyping and prejudice.

Supplies:

You'll need Bibles, one copy of the "Solar Stereotypes" handout (p. 102), scissors, newsprint, markers, tape, paper, pencils, and bread.

Experience:

Photocopy and cut apart the "Solar Stereotypes" handout (p. 102).

Form four groups. (A group can be one person.) Assign each group one of the following roles: Martians, Jupiterians, Saturnians, or Mercurians. Give each group the corresponding handout section.

Say: **You've been invited to plan a party to honor earthlings. In your group, read your role and talk about how you'll act when you begin party-planning. Follow the instructions, and ham it up during the discussion time.**

Give students three minutes to talk about their strategies. Have groups each come up with a "greeting" they'll use to begin the discussion—for example, they may create a rhyme about their planet or beliefs or they may do a few silly motions.

While students are planning, write the following actions on newsprint: (1) Determine who'll be the Note-Taker; (2) Elect a Party Chairperson; (3) Decide on a menu; (4) Prepare seating arrangements; (5) Determine entertainment; and (6) Elect someone to choose and say the opening prayer.

Tape the newsprint to the wall.

Have students sit in a square, with each group making up one side of the square. Have groups present their greetings. Then say: **You're here today to plan a party for your favorite people—the earthlings. You want the best party possible for your friends. The items on the newsprint represent some of the things you'll need to discuss as you plan the party.**

You have six minutes to plan the party. Ready? Go.

Remind groups to stay in character during this activity. After six minutes (or less if the discussion dies down earlier), call time. Have the Party Chairperson (if one was elected) explain what was decided. Ask:

● **How easy was it to get things accomplished in this activity? Explain.** *(Very difficult, people didn't communicate well; impossible, the other groups wouldn't listen to us.)*

● **How did you react to the way you were treated by other groups?** *(It wasn't fair; I was angry; I was upset.)*

● **How is that like the way people react when others show prejudice against them?** *(It's the same feeling; it's more painful.)*

● **How did your prejudices help or hurt the planning process?** *(They hurt the process by stalling discussion; they helped by eliminating groups who didn't have much to offer.)*

● **What does this activity tell us about prejudice?** *(Prejudice makes people feel bad; prejudice keeps people from accomplishing tasks; it's easy to be prejudiced.)*

Say: **Though you've probably heard about the civil rights movement of the '60s and the ongoing problems with racism around the world, you may not know that prejudice existed even in Bible times.**

Read aloud Isaiah 59:8-16a and Micah 6:8. Ask:

● **How does God view injustice?** *(He hates it; he wants it abolished.)*

● **How is prejudice a form of injustice?** *(It limits people's freedoms; it hurts people needlessly.)*

Have volunteers read aloud Acts 10:1-35. Form groups of no more than five. Ask:

● **What did Peter learn in this story?** *(God loves each person regardless of culture, race, or creed.)*

● **Why was Peter prejudiced toward the Gentiles?** *(Because Jews were supposed to be prejudiced; because Gentiles were different from Jews.)*

● **How did God change Peter's prejudice?** *(By teaching Peter that all people are important.)*

● **How are people today prejudiced against the following groups of people: women? homosexuals? Christian or other religious groups? activists for other causes?**

● **Why are people prejudiced today?** *(Because they're uninformed; because they're stupid; because their parents were.)*

Form pairs. Give each pair a piece of bread. Say: **This bread represents the walls of prejudice. By not eating this bread, we're upholding the traditions and ignorance that keep our prejudices intact. Like Peter, we're following the "rules" someone else set up that make us narrow-minded. Take turns with your partner holding the bread and telling** one way you've acted unfairly toward someone. It might be as simple as giggling silently about the way someone was dressed or telling ethnic jokes. Then talk about how you felt when you showed prejudice or how you feel when others are prejudiced against you.

Allow a few minutes for partners to tell each other their experiences. Then say: **Now I'd like both partners in each pair to hold the piece of bread and slowly tear it in half. Then eat your half of the bread, or at least a small part of it. Say a silent prayer, asking God to break down the walls of prejudice so you can see that each person is important and loved by God.**

SOLAR STEREOTYPES

Martians:
- You tolerate the Saturnians, but you think all other life forms are "dweebs."
- You detest the Jupiterians because they love monga soup.
- You'd rather fight than be forced to eat monga soup.
- You pray to the Big Dipper.
- You think Mercurians only like mugbugli music.
- You know you're the best leaders for this committee because you're smarter than everyone else.
- You'd never lower yourselves to be Note-Takers for this meeting.

Jupiterians:
- You know you're superior to all other life forms.
- You'd rather not be at this meeting.
- You know you'd plan a better party without all these "glunks," "glurbs," and "gimlets" (Jupiterian slang for "idiots").
- You love to eat monga soup, and you plan to suggest it for the main course.
- You pray to the Big Dipper.
- You think Martians only like bamboomboom music.
- You wouldn't be caught dead taking notes—that's for lowlifes such as the Mercurians or the Saturnians.

Saturnians:
- You know you're better than Jupiterians, but you respect the other life-form groups.
- You love to eat fried cadbingle, and you plan to suggest it for the main course.
- You think your underwater barbershop-quartet would make wonderful entertainment for the party.
- You'll reluctantly be Note-Takers for the meeting, but you'd rather lead the meeting.
- You think Martians don't know how to read or write.
- You pray to the Little Dipper.
- You think Mercurians only like tinwhallopy music.

Mercurians:
- You know you're superior to Martians and Jupiterians.
- You tolerate Saturnians, except for their love of fried cadbingle, which you think tastes like soggy wallpaper.
- You hope the other groups don't suggest music for the entertainment, because you detest all music.
- You don't want to take notes because you'd get your tentacles dirty.
- You're sure the Martians and Jupiterians are conspiring to take over your planet.
- You pray to the Big Dipper.
- You believe monga soup is only for weaklings; you'd rather have a smerg steak any day.

Wedding Day

Purpose:
Students will learn about the importance of compatibility in marriage.

Supplies:
You'll need Bibles, paper, scissors, pencils, newsprint, markers, and one copy of the "Before You Ask, 'Will You Marry Me?'" handout (p. 106) for each person. Also, photocopy and cut apart the "Verses for Vows" handouts (p. 107) so that every student gets one copy.

Experience:

Cut one slip of paper for each student in the group. Number pairs of slips with matching numbers. (Write "1" on 2 cards, "2" on 2 cards, and so on.) Make a code mark (such as the letter B) on one card in each pair to designate the bride in the couple.

Tell the students that a sophisticated computer-dating service will select students in the group who would make great couples. Randomly distribute the slips of paper. Then tell students about the code. Say: **You must find the person who has the same number as you. Once you've found your match, see who has the "B"** (or the code mark you selected). **That person gets to be the lucky bride!**

Be prepared for bursts of laughter, since the matching may or may not have paired males with females. Say something about modern technology's quirks.

Give couples paper and pencils. Then say: **We're about to find out about some of your quirks, values, and dreams. For the next five minutes, you'll plan as much of your wedding as time allows. Don't pretend to be somebody else. Be yourself, and give your actual opinions. For example, maybe you've thought about having a big wedding, a small wedding, or even eloping. The two of you must decide together what plans you'll make as if the two of you were combining your wishes to plan a real wedding.**

Write the following questions on newsprint, and tell pairs to include the answers to these questions in their plans.
1. How long will your engagement be?
2. When will your wedding be held?

3. Where will your wedding be held?

4. How big will your wedding be?

5. What colors and flowers will you select?

6. Will you write your own vows or use traditional ones?

7. Where will your honeymoon be?

Say: **Write your final plans on your paper. Remember, you're a couple, and you must come to a consensus. Go!**

Pressure students to finish quickly. That will enhance the feeling of frustration.

When couples are finished, ask a few couples to submit their wedding plans. Thank them for their hard work and then form groups no larger than six. Ask:

● **What were your thoughts during this exercise?** *(I felt frustrated; this activity was embarrassing; it was difficult to do this activity.)*

● **How was this activity similar to planning a real wedding?** *(It's not easy to compromise; there was too much to do in too little time.)*

● **What were examples of when you agreed, disagreed, or compromised?** *(We both wanted a big wedding; one of us wanted a big wedding and the other wanted to elope.)*

● **What did this exercise tell you about two people's backgrounds coming together for a marriage?** *(One person may have to give in; people each have their own ideas about how things should be done.)*

Have students each tell what they appreciated about how their partner handled compromising and working together.

Say: **Have you ever heard the phrase "opposites attract"? There may be some truth in that, but most lifelong marriages are built on what partners have in common, not what they disagree about. Sure, it's fine to have some differences, such as one partner preferring winter and the other preferring fall. But there can be real trouble if one is a devoted Christian and the other is a devoted atheist. A starting point for a good marriage is selecting the right person. Let's explore important questions two people must discuss before making marriage plans.**

Give students the "Before You Ask, 'Will You Marry Me?'" handout (p. 106). Have original couples pair up again and iron out the answers to as many questions from one category as they can. If time allows, have couples discuss another category. For variety, assign different couples to different categories.

Ask group members:

● **How'd you feel about discussing those questions with your partner?** *(It felt weird; I felt closer to my partner.)*

● **Why do you suppose so many couples never discuss these questions before they marry?** *(It could be touchy; couples might not want to deal* *with areas they don't agree on; they'd rather get married and work them out later.)*

● **How important is a couple's agreement to these questions for a lasting marriage?** *(Very important; pretty important, people can disagree and still be married.)*

Say: **There's a lot to think about before taking the plunge into a life-long commitment.**

Now it's time to search God's Word for what's important in marriage. I'll give you a list of Bible verses. Look up those verses, and create a wedding vow with your partner. The vow can be a sentence or several sentences. The vow becomes a promise two people make to each other when they commit to marrying each other.

Give students each a "Verses for Vows" handout (p. 107), a pencil, and a Bible. Have pairs complete their handouts and read their vows to the group. Ask:

● **What did you learn about marriage by writing a vow?** *(The Bible can help make a good basis for a wedding promise; it's hard to write a vow.)*

● **What's God's idea of a perfect marriage?** *(Two people becoming one; two people serving each other like Christ serves the church.)*

Say: **While marriage may be a long way off in your life or not even a part of your future, learning what it takes to make a perfect marriage can help you have better relationships with others.**

Before You Ask, "Will You Marry Me?"

Family Questions
- Do you both want children? If so, how many?
- How long will you wait before you have children?
- Would both of you feel good about adopting children if you couldn't have children of your own?
- What's your philosophy about raising children? How would you discipline them? reward them?
- Who will do the cooking? cleaning? laundry? shopping? yardwork? carrying out the garbage? vehicle maintenance?
- How much time should each of you spend with friends?

Faith Questions
- Are you both Christians? How will that affect your marriage?
- How do your families view the Christian faith? the church?
- Do you both come from similar church backgrounds? How may that affect your marriage?
- Will you worship together? How often?
- Will you do family devotions? meal prayers? Bible reading?

Money Questions
- Do you plan to work out a detailed monthly spending budget before you're married?
- What proportion of your monthly income will you put into savings?
- How much money will you give to the church? to charities?
- Should you get permission from each other before you spend any money?
- How do you feel about borrowing money from your parents or other relatives?

Communication Questions
- Do you always believe everything your partner tells you?
- What topics are off-limits because they cause conflict? Is it possible to endure an entire lifetime without dealing with those topics?
- When you have a conflict with your partner, do you typically talk about it, shout it out, clam up, or use physical force? How would your two styles of handling conflict mix in a marriage?
- How much should you know about what your partner does when he or she is away from you?

Save this list of questions. Use them to get better acquainted with a friend who could become a lifetime partner.

Verses for Vows

Read these verses about how God is central to the marriage commitment before you create a wedding vow.

- Genesis 1:27-28
- Genesis 2:23-24
- Matthew 6:19-21
- 1 Corinthians 10:24
- 1 Corinthians 11:11-12
- 2 Corinthians 4:16-18
- Ephesians 4:2-3
- Ephesians 5:21-33

Our Wedding Vow

Verses for Vows

Read these verses about how God is central to the marriage commitment before you create a wedding vow.

- Genesis 1:27-28
- Genesis 2:23-24
- Matthew 6:19-21
- 1 Corinthians 10:24
- 1 Corinthians 11:11-12
- 2 Corinthians 4:16-18
- Ephesians 4:2-3
- Ephesians 5:21-33

Our Wedding Vow

What a Weight

Purpose:

Students will discover what it feels like to be forgiven.

Supplies:

You'll need Bibles, large books, and a chalkboard and chalk or newsprint and a marker.

Experience:

Give students each a large Bible or another large book such as a dictionary. Ask them to keep their elbows straight and hold the books in front of them at shoulder height. Tell students to hold the books as long as they can.

As they are holding their books, have students talk about times they messed up in relationships and how they felt. Periodically, ask students how their arms feel.

After a few minutes, or when students show signs of having sore arms, call time and form a circle. Ask:

● **How difficult was it to hold the weight up?** *(At first it was easy; it got tougher as time went on.)*

● **How did you feel as the book began to feel heavier?** *(Sore; nervous; frustrated.)*

● **How is this like the way you feel when you've done something wrong and you haven't asked forgiveness for your actions?** *(I feel worse by the minute when I don't resolve problems; I begin to feel bad about times I've messed up.)*

● **How did you feel when you were able to put the book down?** *(I felt relieved; I felt good.)*

● **How is this like the way you feel when you've been forgiven for something you did?** *(I feel relieved; I feel good.)*

● **How can this book be compared to sin?** *(It's like a heavy weight that you have to hold up; it feels so good when the weight of sin is taken away.)*

Say: **When we mess up and do things we know aren't right, we begin to feel sin weighing us down. Fortunately, our sins can be forgiven so we can move on with our lives and feel good about ourselves again.**

Give students each a Bible. Say: **Jesus met a woman who was experiencing exactly the kind of weight we've been talking about.** Have a volunteer read aloud John 8:2-5. Ask students to imagine the woman standing in the middle of all of those people. Ask:

● **How do you think the woman in this passage felt?** *(Scared; embarrassed; ashamed.)*

Have a volunteer stand so the rest of the students can see him or her. Give the volunteer several books to hold. Explain that those books represent the weight of the volunteer's own sin. Then have students each come up and hand the volunteer another book. Explain that each of their books will represent a condemnation of that person.

Ask the volunteer:

● **What's it like to stand there with all of those burdens?** *(I feel weighed down; it makes me sad; I feel frustrated.)*

Ask the rest of the group:

● **When have you felt like our volunteer?** *(When things have been going badly; when I've messed up too many times.)*

Have the volunteer set the books down and then read aloud John 8:6-11.

● **Why do you think Jesus began writing in the dirt?** *(To focus attention away from the woman; to show the Pharisees he wasn't going to answer the way they wanted him to.)*

● **What did Jesus tell the people who wanted to stone the woman?** *(Whoever doesn't have any sin can throw the first stone; everyone has sinned.)*

● **What can we learn from Jesus' response to the Pharisees?** *(We shouldn't condemn others; we're all sinners.)*

● **How do you think the woman felt after this experience?** *(Relieved; grateful; hopeful; clean.)*

● **What can we learn from Jesus' response to the woman?** *(Jesus will forgive us; Jesus wants to make us different.)*

Have students read 1 John 1:8–2:2 silently. As they read, randomly write the following words on a chalkboard or a sheet of newsprint: "drunkenness," "premarital sex," "theft," "lying," "cheating," and "profanity."

After a few minutes, have students look at the list. Ask students to think about things they've done that have separated them from God. Then say: **We're all guilty of sin. But when we confess our sins to God, he forgives us and completely cleanses our lives.** Erase the chalkboard or tear down the paper and throw it in a trash can.

Say: **It wasn't easy for God to forgive our sins. Because God is righteous, he couldn't just overlook our sins or pretend they didn't happen.** Ask students to open their Bibles to Hebrews 9:22. Have a volunteer read the verse aloud. Explain that, in the Old Testament, people were instructed to sacrifice animals as a way to repent of their sins. The sacrifices were not perfect and had to be done again and again.

Have another student read aloud Hebrews 9:27-28. Ask:

● **What does this passage tell us about forgiveness?** *(Jesus died for our sins; Jesus was the sacrifice to take away all our sins.)*

Say: **Because we aren't perfect, we sin. But God sent Jesus to die for our sins so we could have a relationship with God even though we didn't deserve it.**

World Council

Purpose:

Students will explore why there is injustice in the world and what they can do about it.

Supplies:

You'll need Bibles, several copies of the "World Council" handout (p. 114), scissors, paper, markers, tape, a "Why Injustice?" handout (p. 115) for each group of four, and pencils.

Experience:

Form six groups. (A group can be one person.) Assign each group one of the fictitious countries listed on the "World Council" handout (p. 114). If your group has fewer than six students, use only as many countries as you have students. Give groups each paper and markers.

Say: **For the next activity, you'll each be representing the country you've been assigned at a World Council meeting. You're meeting today to discuss the injustices in your countries and how they can be confronted. You'll each want the other countries to see your need as the most important need in the council. Only the country with the most serious injustices will be given support from the World Council to help solve the problems. Before the World Council meeting, you'll need to design a flag that represents your country. Use the paper and markers to create your flags.**

Arrange chairs in a circle with members of each "country" sitting near one another. Have countries each tape their flag on a chair or table near them.

Say: **Take a couple of minutes to plan how you'll present your plea for assistance to the World Council. Then each country will have two minutes to make its presentation. As you plan, be sure to think about how you might respond to other countries' claims.**

Distribute the "World Council" handout sections (p. 114) to the appropriate teams. After a couple of minutes for countries to discuss their strategies, call time.

One at a time, have countries each present its case to the rest of the countries. Don't allow any talking during the presentations. After all the presentations, allow countries to react to what other countries said. Act as moderator and allow only one representative to speak at a time.

After a couple of minutes, have a secret election to see which country's problem will be chosen as the one the World Council will deal with. Give students each a sheet of paper and a pencil, and have them write on the paper the name of the country they're voting for. Tell students they can vote for their own countries. Collect and tally the votes to determine the winning country. If scores are tied, add your vote to determine the winner.

After the vote, ask:

● **How did you feel as you presented your case to the council? Explain.** *(Frustrated, I didn't think they'd care about our country's problems; excited, I knew we could convince others about the seriousness of our problems.)*

● **How easy was it to decide which country's injustices were most serious? Explain.** *(It was very difficult, all the problems were serious; it was easy, some problems would be impossible to deal with.)*

● **What can you learn from this activity about injustice?** *(Injustice is difficult to overcome; people have different opinions about what injustice is; all injustice needs to be dealt with somehow.)*

● **Which is more difficult: determining why there's injustice or finding ways to solve injustice? Explain.** *(Solving injustice, because it's difficult to know where to start; determining why there's injustice, because we don't always know what causes it.)*

Say: **Of course all injustice is serious. But as we discovered in this activity, the questions "Why is there injustice?" and "What can we do about injustice?" aren't easy questions. We're going to try to answer them anyway, beginning with "Why is there injustice?"**

Form groups of no more than four. Give groups each a "Why Injustice?" handout (p. 115), a Bible, and a pencil. Have groups each follow the instructions, complete the handout, and discuss the questions at the bottom of the handout.

Have groups each report back to the whole group. Ask:

● **How easy was it to determine the reasons for injustice in each situation?** *(It was very difficult because we didn't know the whole situation; it was difficult because there seemed to be lots of reasons; it was easy.)*

Say: **Just as you may have struggled with completing the handout, we struggle with knowing the reasons injustice occurs. But we know one thing for sure—God is aware of the injustices that occur in our world.** Ask:

● **If God is in control, why doesn't he do something about injustice?** *(He lets us deal with it; he does, through his people; because he wants us to grow and learn from it.)*

● **Does injustice in the world bring us closer to God? Why or why not?** *(Yes, we learn to rely on God more; no, it separates us from God.)*

Read aloud Ecclesiastes 7:13-14 and Romans 8:28. Ask:

● **What do these verses tell us about God's role in our unjust world?** *(God will work for good even when things look bad; God allows both good* *and bad to occur.)*

● **Does God cause injustice to happen? Why or why not?** *(Yes, since he's in charge and it does occur; no, we've messed up and are responsible for what happens.)*

● **Does knowing why injustice occurs help us fight it? Why or why not?** *(No, the reasons don't help us know what to do; yes, we can be more confident in our approaches to injustice.)*

Say: **We don't know all the reasons injustice occurs in the world. But, as it says in 1 Corinthians 13:12, we only see a small part of the picture. God sees the whole picture. We need to trust that God's in control and working his plan for good—even when we can't see the results.**

World Council

Photocopy and cut apart these sections.

Livinia

Situation: There are more than ten thousand refugees in this war-torn country. More than two hundred civilians were recently gunned down in a church they thought was a safe haven.

Albankola

SITUATION: Christians are persecuted and imprisoned for their beliefs. It is believed certain high-level government officials are in charge of the anti-Christian actions.

Usurpasia

Situation: Homelessness and poverty plague the underprivileged classes. Each day, as people throw away millions of dollars in state lotteries, another hundred people lose their homes and move out into the streets.

Roomalia

SITUATION: Handicapped and mentally retarded children are institutionalized, neglected, and given severely inadequate care.

South Tenovia

Situation: Racial discrimination and prejudice run rampant in this country. Every day people are killed in violent uprisings caused by segregation and unfair practices.

DURBANIA

SITUATION: People who refuse to grow marijuana or other similar substances on their farms are being burned out, kidnapped, or killed by drug lords who run the government.

Why Injustice?

Read each of the following situations, and discuss why you think injustice occurred in each situation. Read the associated Bible verses to help you think about why some injustices might occur. Write your answers in the space provided. Then discuss the questions at the bottom of the handout.

● **Situation 1**—The people of Bogo-Bogo work their fields every year. They faithfully plant seeds in holes six feet deep and water them once a week. But there is rarely any growth. So the people suffer from famine in their land. Agricultural experts from other countries offer their services to the Bogo-Bogan government, but the officials won't accept any outside help. The officials are happy as long as there's food on their own tables. Read Acts 9:1-22.

Why is there injustice in Bogo-Bogo?

● **Situation 2**—Just when the people of Ragatan begin to rebuild their hurricane-wrecked homes, their country is hit with a major earthquake. Thousands of people are killed in the second major disaster in less than four months.

Read Genesis 3:17-19.

Why is there injustice in Ragatan?

● **Situation 3**—A luxury liner in the Pacific Ocean is attacked by terrorists. When the demands for millions of dollars in ransom aren't met, the terrorists blow up the ship, killing all its passengers.

Read Romans 5:12; 1 Corinthians 10:24; and Titus 3:3-5.

Why is there injustice on the luxury liner?

Discussion questions:
● How do you feel when you hear about injustice in the world?
● Is it easy to understand why injustice occurs? Why or why not?
● How does knowing the reasons for injustice make it easier or harder to deal with?
● Could ignorance, sin, the fallen world, and Satan be reasons for injustice in the world? Explain.

World Wide Web

Purpose:
Students will explore God's commission to be his hands and his mouth in the world.

Supplies:
You'll need a Bible and a ball of string.

Experience:

Form a circle. Hold up a ball of string, and tell students you're going to create a web. Wrap the end of the string around one hand and then toss the string across the circle with the other hand. Have that person wrap the string around one of his or her hands and then toss the string to someone else in the circle. Continue until a web is formed between all the group members.

One at a time, have students lean back, depending partially on the string to hold them up. As each person does this, have the other students raise their free hands if they can feel the effects of the leaning person on their own section of the web.

After everyone has leaned back, ask:

● **What did it feel like to lean back in the web?** *(I was afraid I would fall; it was fun.)*

● **What did you think as you saw other people leaning back?** *(I wondered if I would have to hold up most of their weight; I wondered if I'd feel the effects in the web.)*

● **How is leaning back in the web like the effects one person can have on the world?** *(The effects of one person's life can be felt worldwide; one person affects one part of the world more than another.)*

● **What are some ways people have "changed the world"—for good or bad?** *(Hitler changed the world by starting a war; Martin Luther King, Jr. changed the world by preaching about racism.)*

● **As a Christian, how can you change the world?** *(I can become a missionary or a politician; I can pray; I can send money to feed the hungry in other countries.)*

Say: **Just as many people felt the effects one person had on this web, so each of us as Christians can have an effect on the whole world by what we do at home. Let's look in the Scripture to see how that might be done.**

Read aloud Matthew 5:13-14. Ask:

● **Why does Jesus call us the salt of the earth?** *(Because the presence of Christians on the earth preserves it from destruction; because we bring the flavor of God to people's lives.)*

● **Why does Jesus call us the light of the world?** *(Because we bring the light of Christ into the lives of people who need him; because we help other people grow in their relationships with God.)*

● **How can we be salt and light to people all over the world?** *(By living the way God wants us to here in our own country; by going over to where the other people live; by praying for them.)*

Read aloud Matthew 28:18-20. Ask:

● **What does it mean to "make disciples" of Jesus?** *(To tell others about Jesus; to teach others to live for Jesus like we do.)*

● **Why do you think this passage is called the "Great Commission"?** *(Because it was Jesus' last command before he returned to heaven; because it tells us what we're supposed to be doing while we're on the earth.)*

Form a circle. Say: **God has already commissioned each of us to be his hands and his mouth in the world. And today we're going to celebrate that commissioning by commissioning each other.**

While standing in the circle, turn to the person on your right and say:

(Name)**, one way you demonstrate that you're the salt of the earth and the light of the world is...**

I hereby commission you to go and change the world for Jesus.

Have him or her repeat the commissioning for the person on his or her right. Continue around the circle until each person has been commissioned.

Yes, No, Maybe So

Purpose:

Students will explore ways of relating to people with AIDS or other serious diseases.

Supplies:

You'll need Bibles, newsprint, and markers.

Experience:

Divide the room into two sections. Designate the first section "Absolutely" and the other section "No Way."

Say: **For this activity I need everyone to stand. I'll read a statement and then you have fifteen seconds to decide whether you agree or disagree with the statement. If you agree, stand in the "Absolutely" section. If you disagree, stand in the "No Way" section. Be ready to defend your decision. No one can stand in the middle. You must either agree or disagree. Be honest. And remember, no put-downs allowed.**

Begin reading the "Yes, No, Maybe So Statement List" (p. 119). Read the items one at a time, and allow the students a few seconds to move to their appropriate areas. After the students have decided where they'll stand, encourage several from each group to explain why they agree or disagree. Allow healthy conversation between the two groups as well. Use their discussion to ask deeper, probing questions without embarrassing anyone.

If all the students migrate to one section and leave the other section empty, select a few students to play the devil's advocate and support the other viewpoint.

Yes, No, Maybe So Statement List

- Teenagers are not really at risk to catch AIDS.
- AIDS is God's punishment on homosexuals.
- A person with AIDS should be treated differently than a person with cancer.
- I would be uncomfortable knowing an AIDS-infected person went to my school.
- It can be unsafe to touch a person with AIDS.
- God would never let me get a disease such as AIDS, cancer, or tuberculosis.
- If I found out a friend of mine had AIDS, I would stop hanging out with him or her as much.
- If I found out a friend of mine had cancer, I would stop hanging out with him or her as much.
- I would be uncomfortable if a person with AIDS spent the night at my house.
- I don't know how to act around people with serious diseases.
- I hate hospitals, doctors, and especially dentists!

After several rounds, ask:

● **What was difficult about this exercise?** *(Trying to determine my real feelings; trying to explain why I decided the way I did.)*

● **How did your feelings during this activity reflect how you feel about these issues in real life?** *(I don't think about it as much in real life; I didn't realize I had such strong feelings about these issues.)*

● **What do you think would be the hardest thing about having AIDS or some other serious disease?** *(Being abandoned by my friends; knowing I could never get well; going through sometimes painful treatments; feeling like God was punishing me.)*

● **How would you react if your best friend told you he or she had AIDS?** *(I wouldn't know what to say; I would want to help them any way I can.)*

Say: **Let's see if we can discover how God would react to knowing someone has a serious disease.**

Form small groups of six or fewer. Make sure each group has a Bible, a large sheet of newsprint, and several colored markers.

Instruct the groups to read Exodus 3:1-10 and Matthew 8:1-3 among themselves. Then tell groups each to draw a mural that illustrates God's attitude toward those who are suffering. Allow time for students to draw and then have each group explain its mural to the large group.

After each group has explained its mural, say: **Even though these murals are all different, the overall message is the same: God cares** about people who are suffering. Ask:

● **How does it feel to know that God cares about those who are suffering?** *(Good; convicting.)*

● **How do your feelings and actions compare to God's in this area?** *(I don't care as much as I could; I'm concerned like God is.)*

● **Why do you think God would care whether people have AIDS or some other disease?** *(Because he loves us; because he created us.)*

Say: **When thinking about issues such as AIDS, it's often easy to get caught up in the controversies surrounding the issue and lose sight of the needs of the individuals. God showed compassion to people suffering all kinds of maladies. We must do the same.**

Indexes

Scripture Index

Topical Index

Group Publishing, Inc.
Attention: Product Development
P.O. Box 481
Loveland, CO 80539
Fax: (970) 679-4370

Evaluation for *STUDENT-LED DEVOTIONS FOR YOUTH MINISTRY, VOLUME 2*

Please help Group Publishing, Inc., continue to provide innovative and useful resources for ministry. Please take a moment to fill out this evaluation and mail or fax it to us. Thanks!

● ● ●

1. As a whole, this book has been (circle one)

not very helpful   very helpful

1   2   3   4   5   6   7   8   9   10

2. The best things about this book:

3. Ways this book could be improved:

4. Things I will change because of this book:

5. Other books I'd like to see Group publish in the future:

6. Would you be interested in field-testing future Group products and giving us your feedback? If so, please fill in the information below:

Name _____

Street Address _____

City _____ State _____ Zip _____

Phone Number _____ Date _____

More Resources for Your Youth Ministry

New Directions for Youth Ministry

Wayne Rice, Chap Clark and others

Discover ministry strategies and models that are working in *real* churches...with *real* kids. Readers get practical help evaluating what will work in their ministries and a candid look at the pros and cons of implementing each strategy.

ISBN 0-7644-2103-4

Hilarious Skits for Youth Ministry

Chris Chapman

Easy-to-act and fun-to-watch, these 8 youth group skits are guaranteed to get your kids laughing—and listening. These skits help your kids discover spiritual truths! They last from 5 to 15 minutes, so there's a skit to fit into any program!

ISBN 0-7644-2033-X

Character Counts!: 40 Youth Ministry Devotions From Extraordinary Christians

Karl Leuthauser

Inspire your kids, introduce them to authentic heroes, and help them celebrate their heritage of faith with these 40 youth ministry devotions from the lives of extraordinary Christians. These brief, interactive devotions provide powerful testimonies from faithful Christians like Corrie ten Boom, Mother Teresa, Dietrich Bonhoeffer, and Harriet Tubman. Men and women who lived their faith without compromise, demonstrated Christlike character, and whose true stories inspire teenagers to do the same!

ISBN 0-7644-2075-5

On-the-Edge Games for Youth Ministry

Karl Rohnke

Author Karl Rohnke is a recognized, established game guru, and he's packed this book with quality, cooperative, communication-building, brain-stretching, crowdbreaking, flexible, can't-wait-to-try-them games youth leaders love. Readers can tie in these games to Bible-learning opportunities or just play them.

ISBN 0-7644-2058-5

Exciting Resources for Your Youth Ministry

All-Star Games From All-Star Youth Leaders

The ultimate game book—from the biggest names in youth ministry! All-time no-fail favorites from Wayne Rice, Les Christie, Rich Mullins, Tiger McLuen, Darrell Pearson, Dave Stone, Bart Campolo, Steve Fitzhugh, and 21 others! You get all the games you'll need for any situation. Plus, you get practical advice about how to design your own games and tricks for turning a *good* game into a *great* game!

ISBN 0-7644-2020-8

Last Impressions: Unforgettable Closings for Youth Meetings

Make the closing moments of your youth programs powerful and memorable with this collection of Group's best-ever low-prep (or no-prep!) youth meeting closings. You get over 170 favorite closings, each tied to a thought-provoking Bible passage. Great for anyone who works with teenagers!

ISBN 1-55945-629-9

The Youth Worker's Encyclopedia of Bible-Teaching Ideas

Here are the most comprehensive idea-books available for youth workers. With more than 365 creative ideas in each of these 400-page encyclopedias, there's at least one idea for every book of the Bible. You'll find ideas for retreats and overnighters…learning games…adventures…special projects…affirmations… parties…prayers…music…devotions…skits…and more!

Old Testament ISBN 1-55945-184-X
New Testament ISBN 1-55945-183-1

PointMaker™ Devotions for Youth Ministry

These 45 PointMakers™ help your teenagers discover, understand, and apply biblical principles. Use PointMakers as brief meetings on specific topics or slide them into any youth curriculum to make a lasting impression. Includes handy Scripture and topical indexes that make it quick and easy to select the perfect PointMaker for any lesson you want to teach!

ISBN 0-7644-2003-8

Order today from your local Christian bookstore, or write: Group Publishing, P.O. Box 485, Loveland, CO 80539.